HONEY AND PRESERVES
FORTNUM & MASON

Honey and Preserves

FORTNUM & MASON
PICCADILLY SINCE 1707

EBURY
PRESS

10 9 8 7 6 5 4 3 2

Published in 2011 by Ebury Press, an imprint of Ebury Publishing

A Random House Group Company

Text copyright © Ebury Press 2011
Recipe copyright © Emma Marsden 2011
Photography copyright © Emma Lee 2011
Images on pages 10, 11, 18, 22, 23, 28, 30 and 34 copyright © Fortnum and Mason 2011

Fortnum & Mason has asserted its right to be identified as the author of this Work in accordance with the Copyright, Designs and Patents Act 1988

All rights reserved. No part of this publication may be reproduced, stored in a retrieval system, or transmitted in any form or by any means, electronic, mechanical, photocopying, recording or otherwise, without the prior permission of the copyright owner

The Random House Group Limited Reg. No. 954009

Addresses for companies within the Random House Group can be found at www.randomhouse.co.uk

A CIP catalogue record for this book is available from the British Library

The Random House Group Limited supports The Forest Stewardship Council®(FSC®), the leading international forest certification organisation. Our books carrying the FSC label are printed on FSC® certified paper. FSC is the only forest certification scheme endorsed by the leading environmental organisations, including Greenpeace. Our paper procurement policy can be found at www.randomhouse.co.uk/environment

To buy books by your favourite authors and register for offers visit www.randomhouse.co.uk

Design: TurnbullGrey
Photography: Emma Lee
Food styling: Emma Marsden
Prop styling: Emma Thomas

Printed and bound in China by C&C Offset printing Co., Ltd.

ISBN 9780091943677

Contents

Introduction	7
Bottled Preserves	9
Honey	25
Light Bites and Starters	37
Main Courses	55
Puddings	75
Bakes	93
Preserves	111
Index	127

Introduction

Preserved foods have been a feature of human existence for thousands of years, from our earliest ancestors, who strove to capture the bounties of Nature for use throughout the long winter. Honey has been found in ancient Egyptian tombs, still delicious and usable after millennia. Fortnum & Mason hasn't been making jams, chutneys and purveying honey for quite that long, but for over three centuries we have been proud to supply superlative preserves to our customers.

Today, once more we have come to appreciate the interest that summer fruits and vegetables can bring to the table, and honey is taking its rightful place in the kitchen as arguably the most ubiquitous of natural products. Fortnum's is at the forefront of the rediscovery of the joy of preserves, with our shelves filled with over three hundred traditionally-made jams, marmalades, jellies, chutneys and pickles in our range, and an impressive selection of honeys, including the much sought-after honey from our own rooftop bees.

This little book celebrates the art of preserving, and the glory of honey. It offers a consideration of man's relationship with sweet and savoury kitchen concoctions, developed over centuries by thrifty housewives and high-powered chefs. The easy-to-follow, but simply delicious, recipes, using these Fortnum's delicacies, are set out for us all to try at home.

So, whether your taste runs to the sweet or the savoury, may I recommend the following pages as a satisfying read and an inspiration to all who have longed to use the contents of their store cupboard jars in new and exciting ways.

Kate Hobhouse
Chairman

Bottled Preserves

A HISTORY OF PRESERVING

Britain's first known sweet and sticky food product was termed, simply, as 'stuff', although its meaning was very different from the connotations of clutter associated with the word today. Created in medieval times, it was made by rendering down mulberries with lemon juice and honey. Thanks to its wealth of pectin, this gloopy concoction perfectly served its purpose: to line the tough pastry base of a Bakewell tart. But it wasn't until many centuries later that food preservation came to the fore.

In 1809, French chef and confectioner Nicolas Appert was lured by the FF12,000 prize promised by the government to the first person to discover how to stop food turning mouldy during transportation. His research involved the bottling and corking of jams and jellies, vegetables and dairy produce, among other food types, which he then plunged into boiling water for varying lengths of time. Happily, it proved an unqualified success. In fact, Appert's invention caught on and the process was patented in England. This way of preserving food was, for a long time, single-handedly responsible for relieving the tedium of the nation's limited diet during the dark days of winter, and disguising elements of a dish that were not at their best. Indeed, as recently as only a generation ago, the main method of livening up plain fare was to serve it with the best of summer's produce preserved in bottles.

If you're new to the world of preserving, turn the page for a potted guide to the range of preserves you can enjoy.

EXOTIC TREATS

Fortnum & Mason has long been associated with foods of the finest quality. When the store first opened its doors in 1707 it introduced the British palate to a wide range of culinary delights. Bags of crystalline sugar, jars of spices and richly coloured vinegars from the West Indies and the Far East were presented alongside baskets of fresh, aromatic Seville oranges, tangerines and lemons shipped from neighbouring Portugal. All this and more was available to customers eager to try their hand at home preserves. Discerning shoppers would scoop up basketfuls of these fragrant and exotic ingredients, taking them home for kitchen staff to place in huge open pans and turn into batches of golden-hued, bitter preserves and fruit- and vegetable-rich chutneys and pickles. These would yield enough jars to last right through to the following year when the fruit came into season again.

A RESPECT FOR TRADITION

Around the middle of the nineteenth century, Fortnum & Mason created its own range of preserved foodstuffs, made on the store's Piccadilly premises, and reflecting what was being done in the kitchens of the British gentry. The best of England's seasonal bounty – picked from the lush orchards of Kent and the rich pastures of the Vale of Evesham – was supplemented with imported ingredients unavailable locally, then bottled and proudly displayed in the food hall.

Jam	This describes a preserve made from either one type of fruit or a mixture, which is combined with sugar and water and cooked to setting point (see page 113).
Extra Jam	This is a mixture of one or more kinds of fruit, sugar and water. The difference between this and jam (above) is that no cheaper fruits, such as apples, can be used to pad out the finished preserve; the only permitted extra ingredient is unconcentrated fruit pulp. The minimum fruit content of extra jam is at the higher level of 450g per 1kg.
Marmalade	Also known as a citrus preserve, this may be obtained from the whole fruit, including the juice and the zest, which is cut into strips that are left in the finished marmalade. The minimum fruit content per 1kg of the finished product is 350g.
Curd	Made with fruit juice, eggs and butter, curds are wonderfully rich, creamy and smooth preserves. Curds have a shorter shelf life than other preserves, so these should be kept in the fridge when freshly made, and once opened.
Jelly	Jellies are made by cooking fruit with water to soften it to a pulp, which is then strained to extract the juice. The juice is then cooked with sugar to create a set preserve.

Pickle	Pickling involves vegetables being preserved and/or flavoured with vinegar. In pickles, the vegetables remain whole or chopped in order to retain a shape (rather than cooked down) and have a tender or just-crisp texture.
Chutney	Deriving from the Hindi word 'catni', this savoury condiment has come a long way from the original (a spicy, paste-like mixture of finely chopped herbs and vegetables). The sour-flavoured accompaniment, made with pummelled herbs and spices, and sometimes coconut and fruit, cooled the heat in curries. It has evolved into a slightly sweeter preserve of seasonal fruit and vegetables, balanced with vinegar and sugar. The ingredients are cooked for a long time until thick, so chutneys tend to be robust in flavour.
Relish	Containing less sugar and vinegar than chutney, relishes have a shorter cooking time, which produces an all-round fresher taste.
Mustard	A condiment made from mustard seeds, which may be left whole to create a grainy paste or can be ground for a smooth texture. Mustards are available in a range of intensities from mild to very hot and may have added flavourings (such as alcohol) for variety.

An 1849 catalogue gives some examples: pickles made with homegrown cabbage, walnut and horseradish; and the then newly-fashionable Piccalilli – the mustard-rich vegetable pickle that became the must-have accompaniment for cold cuts. There was also the more exotic Bombay Mango, Chou Chou, Preserved Green Limes and West India Ginger. Against a background, 160 years ago, of almost unimaginable dietary blandness (even in wealthy households), it was extraordinary for any business to be able to offer such choice.

This made Fortnum & Mason an essential stop in the itinerary of any respectable Briton home on leave from Empire duties overseas, who were nostalgic for such wonderful treats. The 1849 brochure encouraged this by advising customers that 'The jams are kept in a concentrated state, put up in the patent jars for exportation, and will keep for years.'

THE WINDS OF CHANGE

Remarkably, Fortnum & Mason's range of preserves remained consistent for the best part of a century. It was Britons working abroad, stationed in the Far East, who led the shift in the nation's tastes. They brought back new culinary flavours, which, in turn, had a huge influence on how Fortnum & Mason selected and developed new products. Indeed, it was a matter of honour at the store that the changing tastes of customers were reflected and satisfied. In the 1930s, the 'discovery' of fragrant mangoes sparked a plethora of new Fortnum & Mason chutneys: Kasoondi Mango, Pepper Mango, Bur Mango and a sweet, sliced mango chutney for more delicate palates all jostled for shelf space. An exotic American-inspired pickle incorporating baby corn on the cob and a spiced West Indian pickle, resplendent with watermelon rind, also joined them.

TOUGH TIMES

It wasn't all plain sailing for the famous Piccadilly store. With a shift in world affairs and economy, the early twentieth century brought in some challenging trading conditions. The 1914 catalogue features a small range of savoury 'jellies for the table' which were served alongside rich meat dishes. During the First World War packets of manufactured apple jelly crystals appeared in the catalogue and on shelves; 'factory' foods like this were created to provide troops on the frontline with imperishable rations, but soon made their way into shops at home. Made from a combination of apple powder, pectin and sugar, this 'modern' product proved to be a timesaving boost for housewives anxious to continue making preserves while sugar was in very short supply.

During the depression of the 1930s, Fortnum & Mason provided an innovative new range of products to appeal to customers. The expression 'pin money' (the small amount of money wives were traditionally given by their husbands to buy pins and haberdashery) was adopted by the store to brand a new range: Pin Money Pickles. Exactly as the name suggests, they were inexpensive but delicious treats. Fortnum & Mason also introduced another economical range of own-brand pickles with a nostalgic homemade appeal, selling under the 'Homestead' label as a way of expressing solidarity with the nation. Renowned French chef, Escoffier, even contributed a recipe!

THE WAR YEARS, 1939-1945

Wartime rationing not only affected the nation's households, it also had a serious bearing on business throughout the United Kingdom. From 1940 until 1952, sugar was so restricted that jam did not feature prominently in any of the Fortnum & Mason catalogues. The jams that were produced were canned (the most cost-effective method) and were simply called mixed fruit jam. The base of these was made from apples, which was combined with any other inexpensive homegrown fruit, such as pears and plums. One addition to the range in 1940, Marrow and Ginger, was clearly influenced by anticipated shortages. Tons of the imported exotic fruits failed to get through as the British merchant ships carrying such produce were targeted by U-boats whilst crossing the Atlantic. Marrows grow easily and quickly in the British climate, provided they are watered sufficiently, and just a little strong, spicy ginger was required in the preserve to flavour the rather bland and watery-tasting vegetable.

At this time Fortnum's outsourced the manufacture of some preserves as the availability of sugar had become limited due to rationing. The appointed company, Elsenham, continued making them to the very letter of Fortnum's recipes, so that customers still enjoyed the products they loved at the same exacting quality they had always known. The challenge for Fortnum's during this time was creating something special with the decidedly finite selection of ingredients available. Necessity is the mother of invention, and the result of the continuing post-war rationing of sugar was a range of Fortnum's preserves that inventively used raisins, chestnuts and oranges as sweetening agents.

Production of own-brand preserves on the Piccadilly premises stopped in 1939 and was transferred to the company's chocolate factory in Brewer Street in Soho, London. But in the latter stages of the war, production of pickles and chutneys had to cease altogether, and it was only in 1947 that domestic pickles, such as Olde English and Imperial, gradually began to reappear. As the country got back on its feet the store began to expand its selection again, selling French capers from 1950 and, in 1957, reintroducing its popular line of Indian chutneys.

QUALITY FIRST

Respect for centuries-old tradition is very much at the heart of Fortnum & Mason's business. Each part of the process is driven by an ingrained desire for perfection, starting with tracking down and selecting the very best fresh ingredients that will work to conjure Fortnum & Mason's unique flavours.

A SELECTION OF BESTSELLING PRESERVES AND HONEYS

Burlington Marmalade Thin Cut 2	The Earl of Burlington knew a good thing when he saw it – namely the neo-classical architecture of 18th century Italy. He would have approved of this marmalade, too. It has been carefully constructed to offer a fine-cut peel and plenty of pale golden jelly with every spoonful.
Old English Hunt Marmalade Medium Cut 3	The Pytchley Hunt has been well chronicled from the mid 17th century. The traditional pre-hunt breakfast prizes the energy-giving properties of marmalade, and this medium-cut recipe is exactly how they like it.
Sir Nigel's Vintage Marmalade Thick Cut 1	This vintage marmalade was made by Fortnum's in the 1920s for actor-manager Sir Nigel Playfair, who asked for a bitter, thick-cut preserve for his toast. We met his request with this – a marmalade with a deep flavour and chewy peel.
Strawberry Extra Jam Preserve 91	The definitive jam of nursery memory, jam-packed with fruit.
Strawberry & Fortnum's Champagne Extra Jam Preserve 61	A childhood classic meets a proper grown-up treat.
Dark Navy Rum Marmalade Thick Cut 5	This thick-cut marmalade laced with a generous tot of Pusser's British Navy Rum was created to commemorate Vice Admiral Nelson's victory over the French at Trafalgar.
Piccadilly Piccalilli	Our much-loved recipe combines crunchy summer vegetables with a mustardy liquor. Enjoy with a cold meat platter, on riverbank summer picnics or at any time with a plate of humble chips. A stalwart British favourite.
Colonel Skinner's Mango Chutney	This chutney is made to the recipe by Colonel Skinner, who served gloriously in the British Army in India. Originally an accompaniment to hot curries, it now serves equally well with red meats, strong cheeses and pies.
Lavender Honey	Mont Ventoux, once famously climbed by Petrarch 'to see the view', stands guard over Provence. The descendants of the lavender trees that enlivened his ascent provide the nectar for this formidable honey.
Rose Petal Jelly 15	This is a preserve pièce de résistance, made with rose petals grown in a single garden in Oxfordshire. The petals are picked in the evening when they are at their most scented, and transferred the next morning to the jelly. Use with sweet and savoury but sparingly – it is so aromatic that less is easily more.

It still comes as a surprise when people learn that every one of Fortnum's preserves is made in the same time-honoured way: ingredients are simmered in large open pans and stirred by hand. Cooks with a keen eye watch over the evaporation process, so that each element cooks at exactly the right temperature to make the perfect preserve.

The type of sugar used also has a strong influence on the finished result. With marmalades, raw cane sugar yields a brilliant, bright colour and flavour. For a softer, lighter taste, Demerara fits the bill, and for rich, liquorice tones, muscovado is perfect.

POTS OF AWARD-WINNING GOODNESS

The word 'marmalade' originally referred to 'quince jam' (from the Portuguese 'marmelada', derived from 'marmelo', or 'quince'). It was only in the seventeenth century that it came to be applied to a preserve made from citrus fruits. From its early days, Fortnum's was quick to build on this history, with a superlative range of what has become a uniquely British breakfast preserve. The range has enjoyed a boost over the past few years thanks to Fortnum & Mason's affiliation with The World's Original Marmalade Awards, based at Dalemain mansion in Cumbria. The initiative started in 2006 and is led by Jane Hasell-McCosh from Dalemain, whose passion for the bitter preserve runs deep. It's a perfect fit for both parties: a celebration of all things golden and a chance to support small, artisan producers. Those who put forward their jars for entry are required to fit them into the somewhat quirkily named categories – Military, Man-made, Peers & Political are just three examples! But for the overall winner (the 'best in show') there's a truly coveted award: their recipe is recreated and sold by Fortnum & Mason. In 2011 the award for the World's Best Marmalade was won by Lord Henley, whose faithful rendition of an old family recipe was an instant hit with the judges. It has proved equally successful with Fortnum's discerning customers, being the most popular marmalade in the current collection.

JAM TODAY, AS WELL AS TOMORROW

The complexity of some jams is mind-boggling: any number of different fruit varieties can go into just one jar to produce the perfect flavour and texture. Fortnum & Mason's Strawberry Preserve cleverly combines Cambridge Favourite and tiny Tioga strawberries to achieve a texture that spreads evenly over hot buttered toast at breakfast time, or equally well on a Victoria sponge for afternoon tea.

The outstanding Woodland Strawberry Preserve, on the other hand, easily identified as a best-quality jam by its distinctive black label, is made with wild Scottish berries specially grown for Fortnum & Mason and harvested just once a year. The cool Scottish climate gives the picked fruit its unique, matchless floral aroma and taste.

CREATIVITY IS THE PRESERVER'S FRIEND

While the creation of jams is nothing more than marrying together sugar and just-ripe fruit then boiling until it sets, sweet jellies use the very same ingredients but are produced by extracting the essence of pectin-rich fruit first. This culinary method is nothing new and was simply born out of our ancestors initial efforts at preservation. For a savoury version, they discovered all that was required was the addition of vinegar and herbs, too. Times have moved on in terms of equipment, though – originally an upturned stool was used to support a piece of cheesecloth or a clean pair of tights which would be hung over a bowl then filled with the cooked fruit to extract the juice. Nowadays home cooks use a freestanding frame, which can be easily set up on the kitchen counter, and a mesh jelly bag.

PERFECT PARTNERSHIPS

Lemons are the traditional flavouring for fruit curd, where the mouth-puckering sourness of the juice softens when teamed with creamy butter and fresh eggs. This toothsome topping is delicious slathered on warm scones and toasted teacakes. Once tasted, it's easy to see why the Victorians delighted in this sublime preserve and served it readily in tarts and pastries for afternoon tea. Cooks have long known that fruits from the same family work well and have reached for oranges and limes, too. Culinary curiosity has led to discovering that passion fruit and lime are a great match as are a combination of berry fruits, as all are packed with that prerequisite innate tartness.

FROM SEED TO PLATE

It is widely believed that the Romans created mustard by grinding together mustard seeds with grape must, although there are many references to the seeds before this time. Now this palate-tingling sauce has become a culinary choice to lift snacks, lunches and suppers. Everything from beef on a Sunday to a sweet ham and crisp lettuce sandwich is more exciting with a spoonful of this pungent seasoning.

Europe, France, Italy, Germany and Britain have all had success in growing mustard, as it is easy to cultivate and produce. However, it is in France and England that there's stiff competition between the regional ranges. In England, Tewkesbury in Gloucestershire and Norwich in Norfolk are the centres of production.

Across the channel, the main varieties of mustard are named after three areas in which they are produced: Dijon, Bordeaux and Meaux (which also goes under the more romantic name of *moutarde à l'ancienne*). Dijon has a soft, creamy texture and pale yellow colour and provides as much warmth in a salad dressing as it does in a creamy sauce for chicken. Mild, brown Bordeaux, with its sweet herby taste, excels with gutsier feasts of pies and bangers. Meaux, by contrast, with its grainy texture from unmilled, crushed grains, has an earthy delicate flavour and can be stirred into a rich stew just before serving.

Now the range at Fortnum & Mason has edged mustard into the spotlight with an ever-expanding choice that complements any savoury dish.

THE MODERN-DAY FACE OF FORTNUM'S

Although tradition underpins Fortnum's preserves, with most staying true to their original recipes, certain accommodation has been given to the changing tastes of the twenty-first century. Key calendar events are now acknowledged. Seasonal offerings include Fortnum's Christmas Curd, which is a clever blend of sharp red strawberries, cranberries and spices offset by mellow seasonal spices.

For chutneys, the fruits and vegetables are specially selected from the season's best and are all prepared and chopped by hand. Sugar certainly plays its part, but it is the vinegar that dictates the flavour: Fortnum & Mason eschews all use of spirit vinegars. A good condiment should work as a bit part in the feast rather than overpower a dish. In this respect, the creative brains behind the recipe development demand that only wine or cider vinegars are used to provide a soft balance of flavour. These work seamlessly alongside all the other ingredients in the chutney, rather than overpowering them.

Fortnum's Piccadilly Piccalilli famously adheres to its authentic roots and still takes centre stage even as new chutney upstarts cluster around it. Newcomers include delights such as Florentine Fruit & Nut Chutney, which is a nod to those who enjoy fruitcake with their cheese! Fortnum's Pickle, fast becoming one of the store's bestsellers, was developed to go with the traditional ploughman's

22 Honey and Preserves at Fortnum & Mason

lunch, and bursts with the flavours of root vegetables cooked down with cider and wine vinegar. From the Spanish classic, membrillo, made with quince, came the idea of developing a range of fruit cheeses to enjoy at the end of a meal: Damson Cheese, made with British fruit, is one such harmonious partner for classic Stilton.

But it is the hardworking sweet-and-savoury jellies that boast countless culinary uses and really earn their place in the kitchen storecupboard. Spread on toast in the morning or on a teacake in the afternoon, and equally handy for taking the edge off a bitter sauce or gravy (just stir in a spoonful as it bubbles away on the hob), they also transform a humble plate of cold cuts or a simple salad.

All Fortnum & Mason's preserves and marmalades are numbered, according to the company taxonomy, within 'The Jam Temple'. (This pedimented fixture is located on the ground floor and holds all of Fortnum's preserves and marmalades, which are displayed in a frieze in numerical order.) This arrangement allows the buying team to keep a close eye on their goods, as it is fundamental to the company's philosophy that Fortnum's offers today's customers the same wide and distinguished range of chutneys and preserves that have been made since 1707. Then, as now, the aim is to preserve the best of the past and marry it with the tastes and appetites of modern-day gourmets.

Bottled Preserves   23

LIQUID GOLD

From the heart of London comes a unique honey produced exclusively by Fortnum's – or, more accurately, by Fortnum's bees. The aptly named 'Fortnum's Bees' is the delightful output from the hives on Fortnum & Mason's Piccadilly rooftop. With a view across the city as far as Norman Foster's 'Gherkin', a colony of bees goes gently about its business from their majestic neo-classical hives, gathering nectar in London's green oases to make one of the world's most natural and ancient foods. Fortnum's Bees Honey is just one of a vast array of fragrant and delicious honeys in store – there's a flavour to please every palate.

According to aficionados, there are two categories of honey, each determined by the plants from which the bees gather nectar. When their route takes in one type of plant only (if the hives are sited in a vast lavender field, for instance), the result is known as monofloral honey and it will have the distinct flavour and aroma of that particular plant. Conversely, when bees gather nectar from diverse flora with a wide range of pollens, the result is polyfloral honey, which produces a more complex flavour.

Honey comes thick set and cloudy, or clear and liquid, the difference in texture depending on the balance of fructose and glucose. Clear, liquid honey contains more fructose, whereas honey with more glucose will crystallise and thicken. But, cannily, there's a way to transform a jar of cloudy honey to its liquid state without affecting flavour or quality. Just place the jar in a bowl of warm water and wait for an hour. Both the thick creamy-textured honey and the clear can be used in baking and cooking, as the recipes in this book testify. For dressings and dishes where the honey needs to dissolve quickly, select the liquid honey, which will amalgamate with the other ingredients and absorb into the mixture easily.

FORTNUM'S HONEY THROUGH THE YEARS

English honeycomb was the only type available in store during the eighteenth and early nineteenth centuries; over time, though, a rich assortment began to be imported from other countries, including golden-hued jars from Greece, Turkey and Provence, famous for the fragrant variety of its wild flowers.

Until 1926, honey was supplied to the store in gigantic vessels, very similar to the way tea and coffee is presented at Fortnum's today. Customers would choose what they wanted, then watch it being decanted into smaller, more manageable jars at the counter.

Sardinian honey was particularly prized – not only for its flavour, which derived from the nectar and pollen of unique indigenous herbs growing wild on the island, but also for the way in which it was collected. To say it wasn't for the fainthearted is an understatement: the hives were perched in inaccessible and often dangerous places, such as the top of the tallest trees, so honey gatherers literally risked their lives to collect it.

In the mid-nineteenth century, a curiosity went on sale in Fortnum & Mason that caused a flurry of excitement in the press, with journalists eagerly travelling from far and wide to report on the new sensation. The honey in question was completely translucent and an unprecedented rose colour; but most intriguing of all, it was manufactured artificially in a production process that Fortnum & Mason determinedly kept secret. Fortnum's windows, lit completely by gas, drew crowds of passers-by curious to view the colour of this unique honey, sparkling in its glass containers. To satisfy public fascination, a jar was sent to the Kensington Museums (later the Science, Natural History and Victoria & Albert Museums) to be displayed for posterity. But the jar disappeared with much speculation as to its fate. Chief among the suggestions was that the curators may have enjoyed several rather fine feasts of honey, toast and tea…

GROUND-BREAKING HARVESTING TECHNIQUES

Extraction techniques moved on apace in the nineteenth century. Collecting the sweet nectar from the racks of the hives had previously entailed smoking out the bees and breaking down the racks, which frequently resulted in colonies being killed. Fortnum & Mason was ahead of its time in terms of environmental awareness, and the store's 1849 catalogue proudly declared that 'Fortnum & Mason has much pleasure in stating that all their Honey has been collected in their improved top hive, without destroying the Bees, consequently the Honey is much superior than when taken in the customary manner, by suffocation.'

SWEET FLAVOURS OF AMBROSIA

With a combined texture of luscious syrup and waxy silk, honeycomb is a delicacy like no other. The wax, built on the wooden frames that the beekeepers lower into the hives, is the other natural product made by the bees and the one that secures their precious golden elixir. At harvest time, rather than spinning the frames to extract the honey, the comb – as it's known in the trade - can be cut out with the honey still attached. This brings no harm to the bees; these productive little creatures simply set to work and rebuild it again once the frame is replaced. Enjoy the comb spread on toast or cut into small pieces with creamy textured Greek yogurt and a spoonful of tart summer berries.

THE AUTHENTIC TASTE OF LONDON

The notion of harvesting honey on the top of a roof on Piccadilly may seem romantic, but behind the fanciful idea lay a curious thought: what would honey produced in the middle of the capital actually taste like? Fortnum's grocery buyer first floated the idea, spurred on by the intriguing supposition that with the wealth of flora in the neighbouring Royal Parks, the honey could end up incorporating myriad wonderful flavours.

With a keen interest in history and a meticulous eye for aesthetic detail, he came up with several sketches for palatial hives that had both architectural merit and an element of fun. These he handed over to a carpenter in Wales. Each was to have its own unique features echoing Roman, Mughal, Chinese and Gothic architectural styles and mirror the eighteenth-century attitude to architectural excellence.

The drawings reveal a fabulously grand design, tall and elegant and far removed from the hitherto squat shape of traditional hives. The roof reflects the regality of the buildings, styled in the shape of a pagoda and crowned with a finial based on woven bee skeps (the old-fashioned dome-shaped hives traditionally made from straw). A triumphal arch at the base embellishes the entrance used by the bees.

The hives are made from stout English oak that will withstand the test of time. Their roofs are sheathed in copper with the finials gilded with real gold leaf, sparkling extravagantly in the reflected light. Steel rods run through the corners of each hive to maintain a rigid framework – particularly useful in high winds. Naturally, they are all painted in Fortnum & Mason's elegant eau de nil.

With the stately apiaries assembled and ready for occupation, next came the question of what type of bee should be invited to take up residence therein. Initially, it was a colony of Carnolian Italian bees, but after a disappointing harvest of a mere 100 jars in the first season, this was reconsidered. Given the intention of conducting tours to the top of the building to view the hives, the next variety had to be friendly, hardworking and, above all, not known to swarm. The attributes of the native Welsh Blacks fitted the bill and have proved to be a stellar success ever since.

In order to let the bees gradually grow accustomed to the hustle and bustle of London life, it was decided that they should progress in a slow, stately manner to the capital in the comfort of their new, majestic homes. The journey began in 2006 when the hives were sited in the grounds of Leigh Manor in rural Shropshire, surrounded by heather bushes; the following year their home became an English garden in rural Oxfordshire, where they could feast on nectar from blousy English roses (the very same flowers, in fact, that are used to produce Fortnum's Rose Petal Jelly). The bees were finally transferred to their London abode in 2008, where they have been in residence ever since. Fortnum & Mason's beemaster presides over their welfare, ensuring that the hives are pristine in the interests of honey production. During winter hibernation, he keeps a watchful eye on the thermometer to make sure that conditions are optimal for the slumbering residents.

Bee lovers can view the comings and goings at the hives via Fortnum's webcam. Links on the website (fortnumandmason.com) connect to beecams 1 and 2, positioned to monitor different aspects of the bees' flight during warm summers when they are at their most active. Regular visitors will occasionally spot the presence of the beemaster on the rooftop tending to the hives.

WHERE THERE ARE BEES, THERE'S HONEY

Fortnum's Bees honey is usually harvested twice a year (weather depending): once the bees have filled the hexagonal wax cells on the racks of honeycomb hanging in each hive, the frames are lifted out and placed in a centrifuge to spin and extract the golden nectar. This filtering process removes impurities before the honey is poured straight into jars to be labelled. You have to be pretty quick off the mark to purchase a jar of the store's own honey, as it is understandably a much sought-after delicacy.

There is endless debate among aficionados as to whether city or country honey delivers the best flavour. Ironically, there seems to be a strong lobby for the former, on the grounds that cities tend to have greater abundance of herbs and flowers to provide the sugary nectar from which bees make honey. This is certainly true of the store's rooftop colony: the bees gather nectar from within a three-mile radius, including neighbouring Green Park, St James's Park, Clarence House and Buckingham Palace, whose grounds are vast and diverse. The tastings certainly attest to this: Fortnum's Bees Honey is richly golden and very runny; its flavour subtly changes from year to year but, due to the many lime trees nearby, it tends to be underpinned by a consistently floral, almost tropical taste, with hints of lychees and a slightly bitter background.

A WIDE VARIETY OF HONEY, EVERY ONE UNIQUE

Establishing its own hives was part of a greater project to ensure that Fortnum's consistently has the best range of honey to offer its customers. A choice number of British honeys form the mainstay of the selection, along with other honeys that are fascinating or distinctive. The collection is sourced from counties

around Britain, so there is variety and a point of difference in every one, whereby the honey provides a unique flavour profile according to the flora in a particular area.

To complement the home-produced range, there are also honeys gathered from countries further afield. For example, Pitcairn Island Honey comes from Pitcairn Island, situated 8000 kilometres from New Zealand. Here is a paradise in its truest form; there are no cars, airports, industry or pollution. The bees forage naturally on an amazing array of wild flowers, none of which have ever been tainted by fertilisers or chemicals. The honey produced is richly scented and intense – a true reflection of the flora and fauna on which the bees feed. In addition, there is also Manuka Honey in the range and this is in a class of its own. Produced on New Zealand's south island, the bees feed on the star-shaped white blossom of the Manuka bushes and produce a chestnut-brown treat with a crystallised texture unlike any other honey. Some compare its rich flavours to wood and eucalyptus, while others associate it with molasses and dried fruit. Whichever camp you fall in, there's big support for its health-giving properties. The unique selling point of this star of the liquid nectar world is its naturally-occurring UMF® (Unique Manuka Factor) 10 factor. This is not found in any other type so it is a one-off in the world of honey and is applauded for its antibacterial quality, which isn't affected by sunlight or heat.

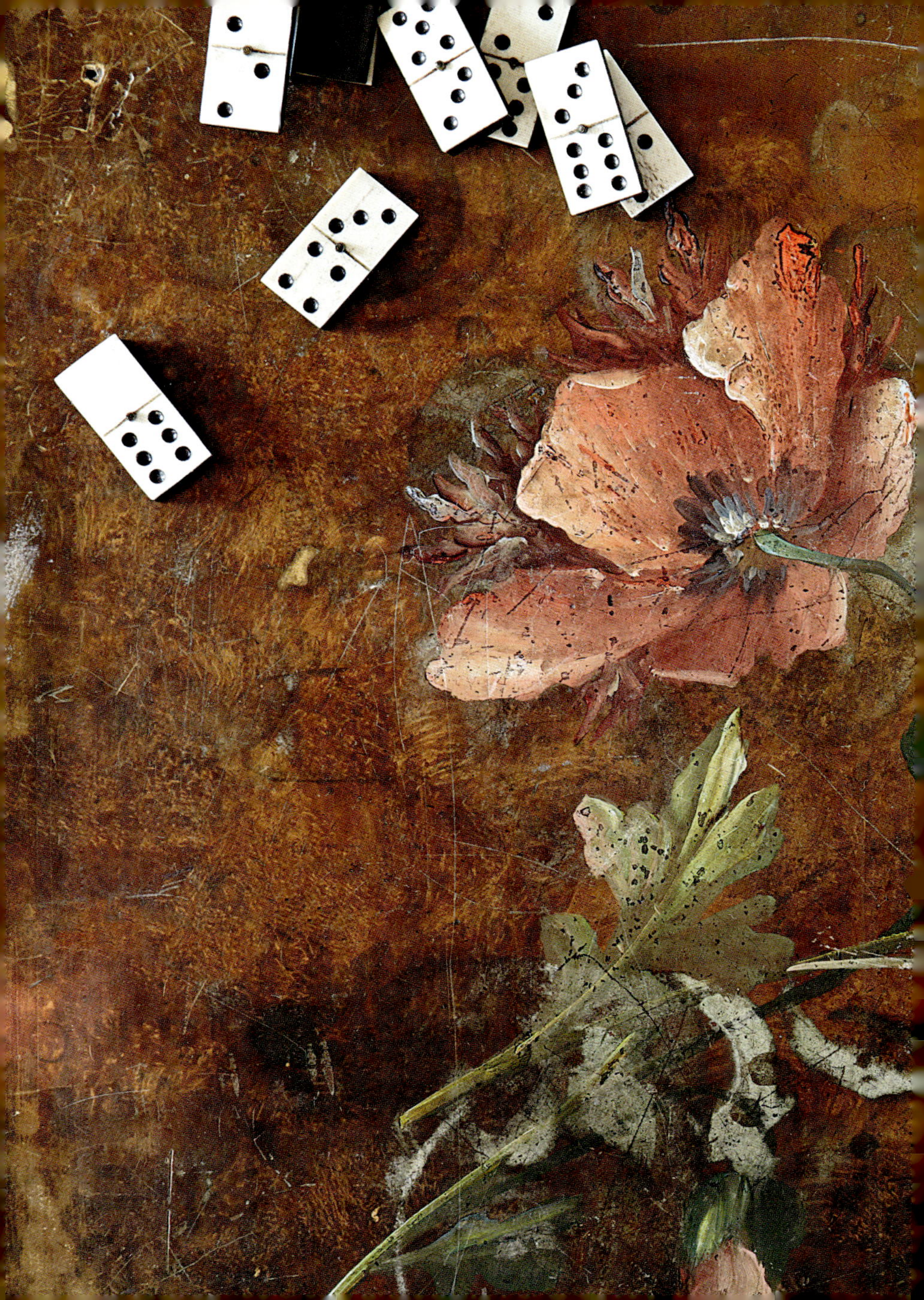

Light Bites and Starters

Parsnip and Thyme SOUP

Borage honey, known for its savoury, cucumber-like flavours, is perfect for this recipe. It emphasises the earthy, natural sweetness of parsnips to create a wonderfully warming, wintry soup. Once blended with the cannellini beans, the dish takes on a comforting silky smooth texture. Garnish with a punchy dressing and vegetable crisps.

Serves 6

2 tbsp olive oil

1 onion, finely chopped

500g parsnips, peeled and chopped

1 tsp Fortnum & Mason runny honey

400g can cannellini beans, drained and rinsed

1.4 litres hot chicken or vegetable stock

1 thick, bushy thyme sprig, plus extra to serve

Salt and freshly ground black pepper

Root vegetable crisps, to serve

For the dressing

1 tbsp extra virgin olive oil

1 tsp white wine vinegar

1 tsp Fortnum & Mason runny honey

Heat the oil in a large pan and cook the onion over a medium heat until softened and beginning to turn golden. Add the parsnips and honey and continue to cook for a few minutes until the edges of the parsnips soften.

Add the beans, hot stock and thyme sprig and season well. Cover and bring to the boil. Simmer for 15–20 minutes until the parsnips are soft. Cool a little.

Whiz the soup in batches in a blender until smooth. Return to the pan and reheat gently.

Meanwhile, for the dressing whisk together the oil, vinegar and honey and season. Ladle out the soup among six bowls. Drizzle the dressing in a circle over the soup. Serve with a handful of root vegetable crisps and garnished with a sprig of thyme.

Pecorino, Courgette, Pine Nut and Rocket Salad

A chunk of mild, salty pecorino cheese is traditionally served drizzled with honey as a starter in Italy. Here this classic combination features in a fresh-tasting salad, beautifully balanced with other favourite Italian ingredients – pine nuts, rocket and courgettes.

Serves 6

2 small courgettes

50g rocket

25g pine nuts, toasted

A small handful of flatleaf parsley, roughly chopped

75g pecorino cheese

For the dressing

3 tbsp extra virgin olive oil

1 tbsp Fortnum & Mason runny honey

1 tbsp wholegrain mustard, such as Fortnum & Mason Hereford Mustard

Juice of ½ lemon

Use a mandolin or a very sharp knife to slice the courgettes into paper-thin rounds. Put them in a large bowl and add the rocket, pine nuts and parsley.

Put the olive oil, honey, mustard and lemon juice together in a bowl and season well. Whisk everything together. Pour over the salad and toss to coat all the ingredients.

Arrange the dressed salad among four plates, then use a vegetable peeler to slice shards of pecorino all over each. Serve immediately.

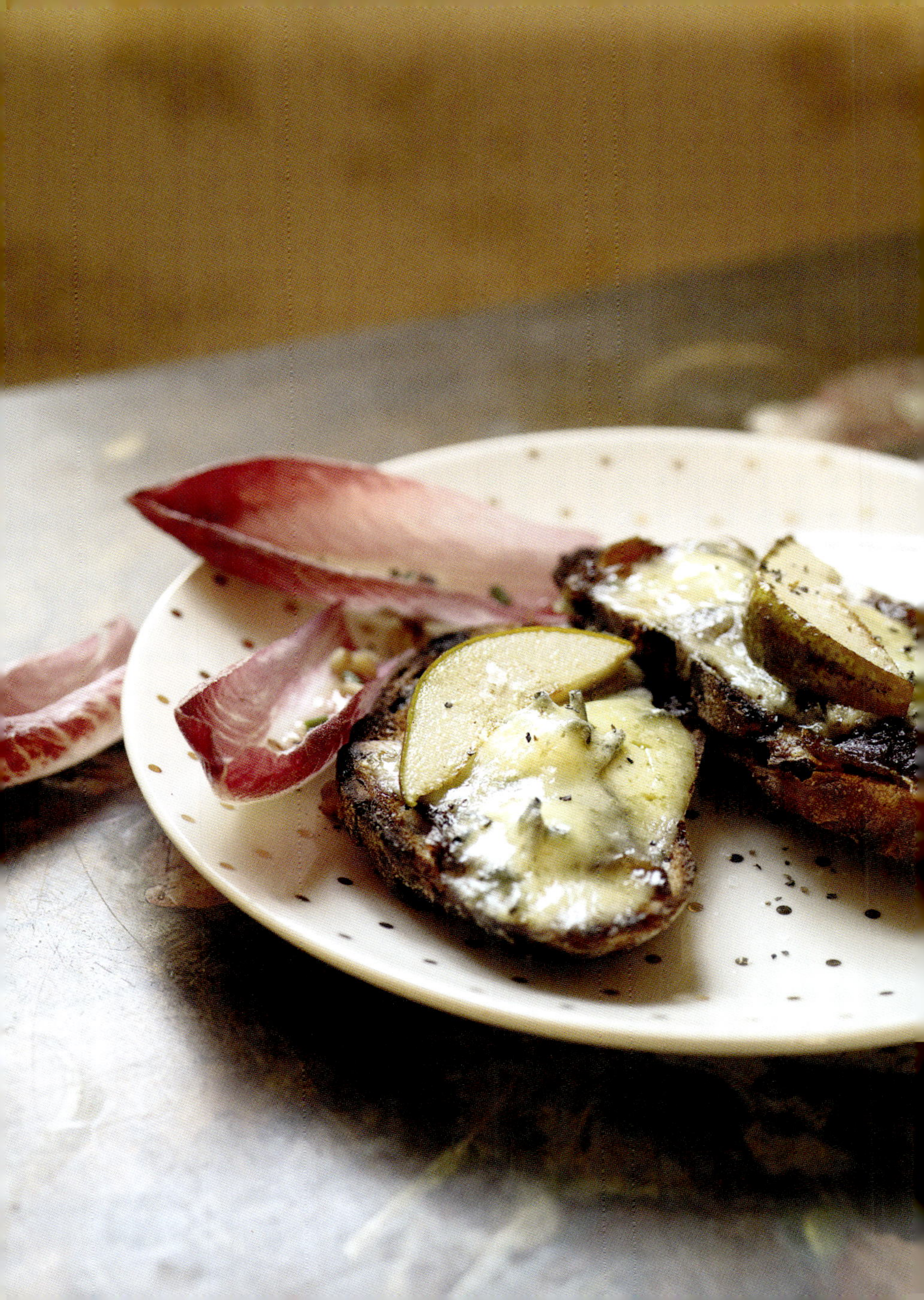

Pear and Stilton
BRUSCHETTA WITH CHICORY SALAD

The textures and flavours of pear and Stilton create a perfect partnership, and here they contrast beautifully with crunchy bread and crisp chicory. Make sure the pears are only just ripe – it will add a little tartness to the finished dish.

Serves 4

A knob of butter

2 pears, halved, cored and sliced

4–8 slices walnut bread, lightly toasted

A little Fortnum & Mason Caramelised Onions

Around 75g Stilton

Salt and freshly ground pepper

For the salad

2 chicory heads

25g walnuts, toasted and chopped

1 tbsp finely chopped chives

2 tbsp walnut oil

2 tbsp red wine vinegar

For the salad, separate out the chicory leaves and put in a salad bowl with the walnuts and chives. Whisk together the walnut oil and vinegar and season. Pour the dressing over the salad and toss well.

Melt the butter in a frying pan and sauté the pears until golden. Season well with salt and freshly ground black pepper.

Preheat the grill. Place the lightly toasted walnut bread on a flat baking sheet and spread each piece with a little of the Fortnum's Caramelised Onions. Top with Stilton and grill until golden.

Divide the bruschetta among four plates, top with the pan-fried pears, and serve with the salad.

Homemade Gravadlax

Homecured salmon is a delicious treat and is ideal for feeding a crowd. This recipe needs to be made several days in advance to allow the salmon time to cure, so it is a wonderful prepare-ahead dish. The sauce can also be done at the same time, just add the dill before you serve so that it keeps its vivid fresh green colour.

Serves 6

- ½ tsp fennel seeds
- 1 tsp black peppercorns
- 1½ tbsp sea salt
- 2 tbsp demerara sugar
- 350g fresh side of salmon, with its skin on
- 10g fresh dill, finely chopped

For the sauce

- 10g dill
- 4 tbsp sunflower oil
- 2 tbsp white wine vinegar
- 2 tbsp Fortnum & Mason Whisky Mustard
- 1 tbsp Fortnum & Mason runny honey or demerara sugar

To serve

Soda bread or rye bread

Place the fennel seeds and black peppercorns in a pestle and mortar with a little bit of the salt and work everything together until the mixture is coarsely ground. Add the remaining salt and sugar and work again to create a coarse mixture.

Line a chopping board with clingfilm – enough to wrap round the salmon several times. Place the salmon in the middle, skin-side down, and sprinkle over the salt mixture to coat it evenly, then cover with the dill. Wrap up well. Place the fish in a container and weight it down with cans, then put it in the fridge. Leave to cure for at least 48 hours or up to five days.

When ready to serve, mix together all the ingredients for the sauce in a bowl with 1–2 teaspoons boiling water. This helps to bring it together.

To serve, unwrap the salmon and place it skin-side down on a board. Using a sharp fish knife, carve very thin slices from the salmon and arrange them on a platter. Serve with the sauce and the bread.

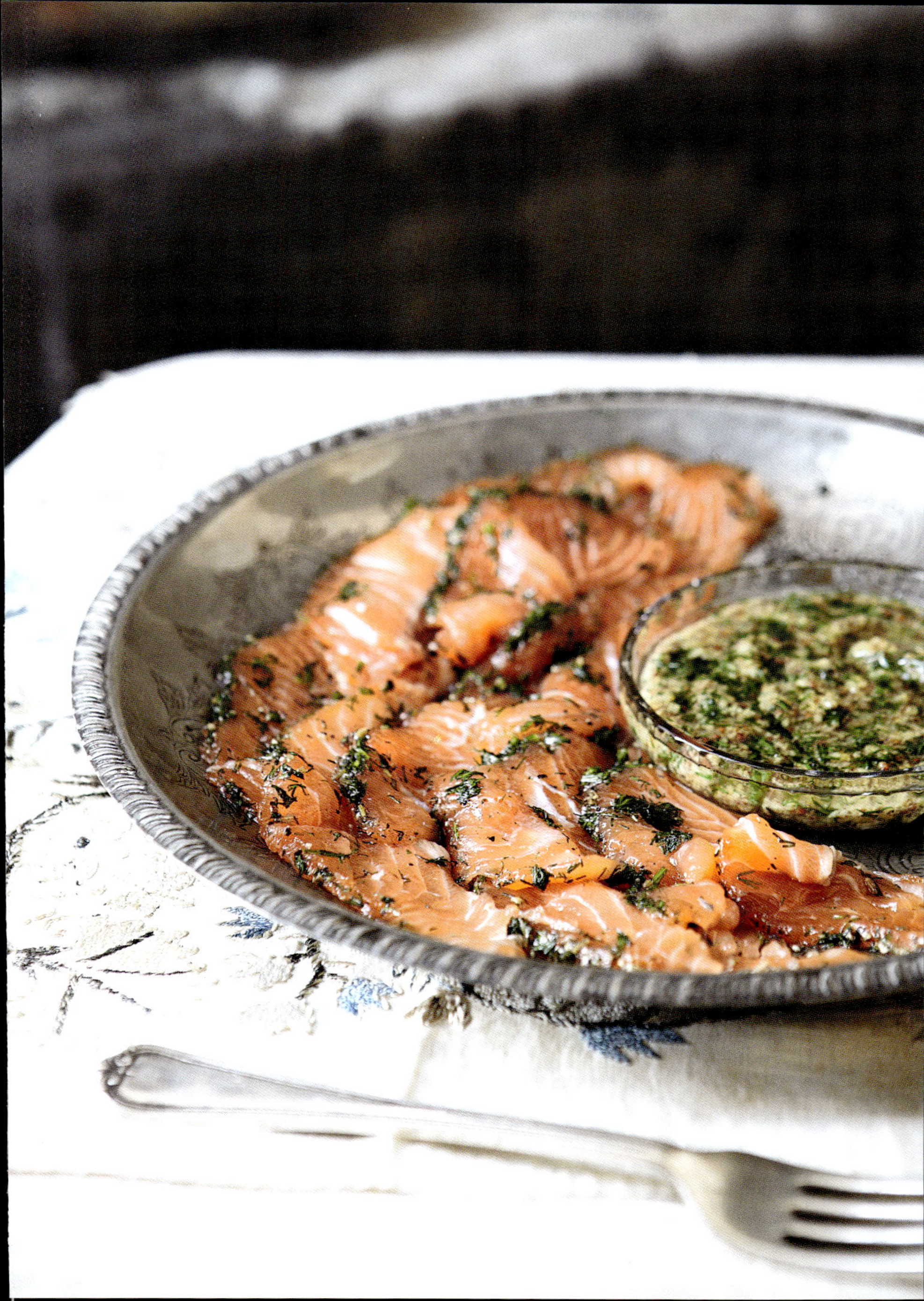

Game and Pistachio
TERRINE

This meat terrine, made with pork belly, rabbit, pheasant, all wrapped in bacon, is studded with pistachio nuts and succulent dried apricots. Team those robust flavours with one of Fortnum & Mason's pickles, such as Piccadilly Piccalilli, for a perfect balance of flavours.

Serves 8

240g rindless streaky bacon rashers

340g pork belly, minced

300g rabbit, minced

25g shelled pistachios

1 tsp salt

3 thyme sprigs

2 shallots, finely chopped

1 tsp ground white pepper

Around 8 dried apricots

2 pheasant breasts

To serve

A selection of Fortnum & Mason chutneys, pickles and pickled vegetables, such as Apricot Chutney or Piccadilly Piccalilli, cornichons and capers

salad leaves

fresh bread

Preheat the oven to 150°C/300°F/gas mark 3. Line a 900g loaf tin with the rashers of bacon, each slightly overlapping the previous one. There should be around five rashers remaining.

Place the minced pork into a bowl. Add the rabbit, pistachios, salt, thyme and shallots. Add the white pepper and mix everything together well.

Place half the mixture into the lined loaf tin and level with the back of a spoon. Arrange the apricots down the middle of the tin. Slice each pheasant breast in half lengthways and lay two halves either side of the apricots. Put the remaining pork mixture on top and level. Cover with the remaining bacon.

Cover with a piece of greaseproof paper, then with foil. Place it in a roasting tin and pour boiling water half way up the sides of the loaf tin. Transfer to the oven and cook for around 1½ hours until the terrine feels firm. It's ready when you insert a skewer into the centre and it is piping hot.

Remove from the roasting tin and cool on a wire rack. Wrap in clingfilm, then weight down and chill overnight.

To serve, unwrap the clingfilm, take off the greaseproof and upturn onto a plate. Slice and serve with chutney, cornichons and capers, a green salad and some bread.

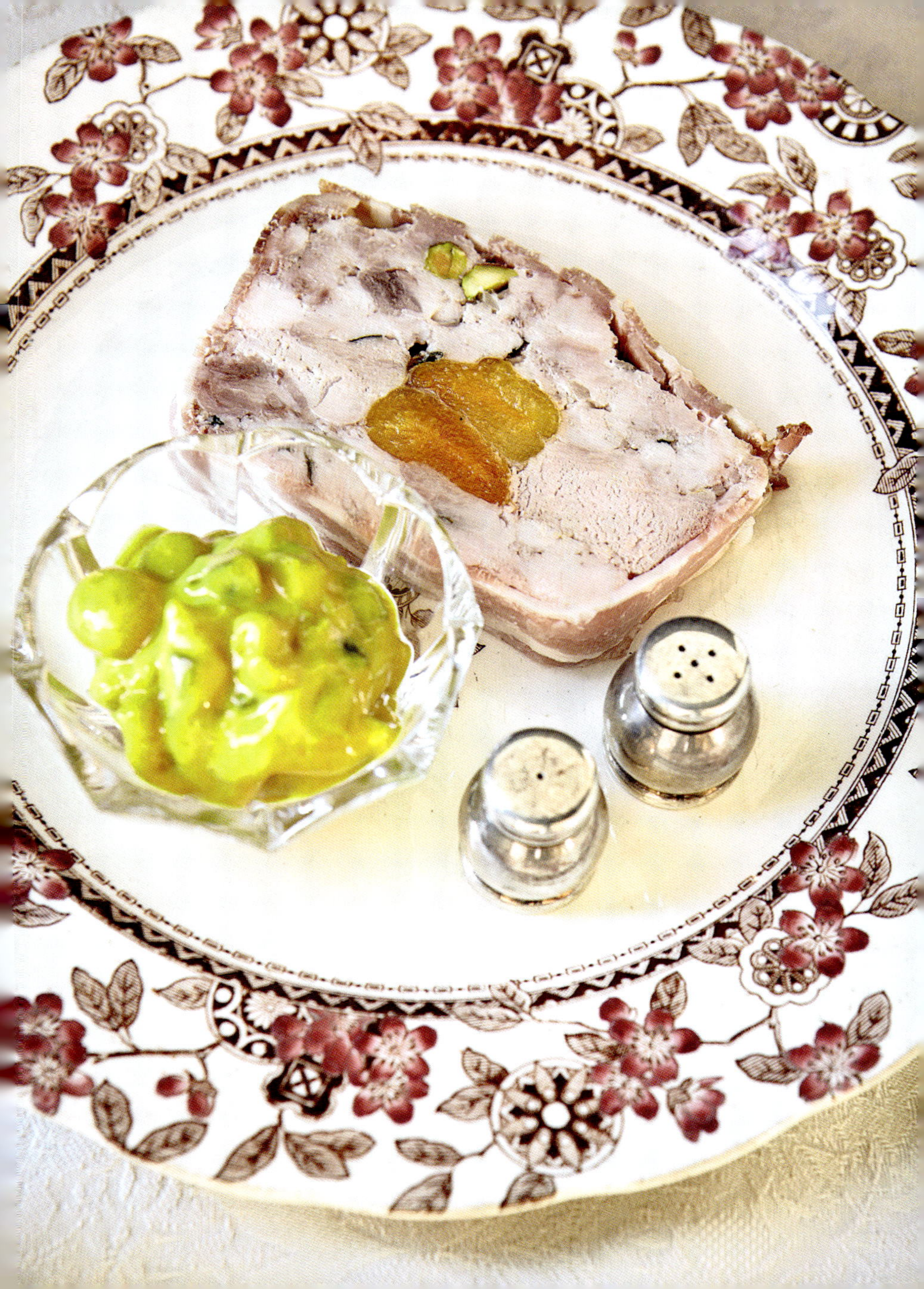

Spinach and Squash
TERRINE WITH PEPPER RELISH

A feast for the eyes and the palate, this stunning terrine features vegetables in a rainbow of colours. It is wonderful served with fresh sourdough or crisp wheat crackers, and garnished with sprigs of fresh watercress.

Serves 8

450g butternut squash, peeled and chopped

400g baby leaf spinach

100g ricotta cheese

2 medium eggs, separated

20g parsley, roughly chopped

Freshly grated nutmeg

Salt and ground white pepper

For the relish

2 red peppers, halved

1 shallot, finely sliced

1 tsp Fortnum & Mason runny honey

2 tbsp olive oil

A squeeze of lemon juice

Salt and freshly ground black pepper

Preheat the oven to 190°C/375°F/gas mark 5. Line a 900g loaf tin with baking parchment.

Steam the butternut squash until just tender, then set aside to cool. Wash the spinach in a colander, put it in a pan and cook until wilted. Cool.

Place the cooked squash in a food processor with half the ricotta, one egg white and the two egg yolks. Season well, then whiz to make a purée. Spoon into the loaf tin.

Rinse out the food processor, then add the spinach, parsley, remaining ricotta and the egg white. Season with salt, white pepper and a little nutmeg. Whiz to make a purée. Spoon on top of the squash mixture.

Cover with a sheet of baking parchment, then with foil. Place in a roasting tin and pour enough boiling water to come halfway up the sides of the tin. Cook in the oven for 45 minutes. Cool on a wire rack.

Meanwhile, make the relish. Preheat the grill to hot and grill the peppers until blackened. Pop them in a bowl, cover and set aside – this steams the skins off the flesh. Once cool, peel the peppers, discarding any core. Slice thinly and place in a bowl with the shallot, honey and olive oil. Add a squeeze of lemon juice to taste and season. Remove the terrine from the tin and upturn onto a plate. Slice, then serve with a spoonful of relish around the outside.

Spicy Crab Salad

A light starter with a real kick. Although crab meat has a delicate taste, it can hold its own with stronger flavours. This colourful salad packs a punch with a sweet and spicy dressing using Fortnum's Scottish Heather Honey.

Serves 4

2 Little Gem lettuces, roughly chopped

6 radishes, finely sliced

½ avocado, diced

1 prepared crab, white and brown meat

1 tbsp finely chopped chives

1 lime, cut into wedges, to serve

For the dressing

2 tbsp extra virgin olive oil

2 tsp white wine vinegar

2 tsp Fortnum & Mason Scottish Heather Honey

A couple of dashes of Tabasco

1 shallot, finely chopped

Salt and freshly ground black pepper

First, make the dressing. Combine all the ingredients in a small bowl and season with salt and freshly ground black pepper. Set aside.

Divide the lettuce among four bowls. Top with the radish, avocado and crab. Drizzle over the dressing, garnish with the chives and serve each with a wedge of lime to squeeze over.

Light Bites and Starters

Pan-fried Scallops
WITH HONEY, SOY AND CHILLI

Scallops, with their natural sweetness and soft melt-in-the-mouth texture, marry well with the hot and spicy tastes of Asian-style ingredients. The inclusion of Fortnum & Mason honey in the dressing adds a delicate sweetness, while spring onions and mint create a refreshing finish.

Serves 4

1 tbsp Fortnum & Mason runny honey

2 tbsp soy sauce

Juice of 1 lime

1 tbsp toasted sesame oil

20 scallops, without roes

1 fresh red chilli, seeded and chopped into fine shards

1cm piece fresh root ginger, chopped into shards

2 tbsp peanuts, toasted and finely chopped

1 spring onion, finely sliced

Salt and freshly ground black pepper

A few mint sprigs, to garnish

Mix together the honey, soy sauce and lime juice, season and set aside.

Heat the oil in a frying pan. Season the scallops then fry in batches for 1 minute only on each side until golden and caramelised. Remove to a warm plate and keep warm.

Add the chilli and ginger to the pan and stir-fry very quickly until just golden. Divide the scallops among four plates, top with the chilli and ginger mixture, the peanuts and spring onion, then drizzle over the dressing. Garnish with the mint.

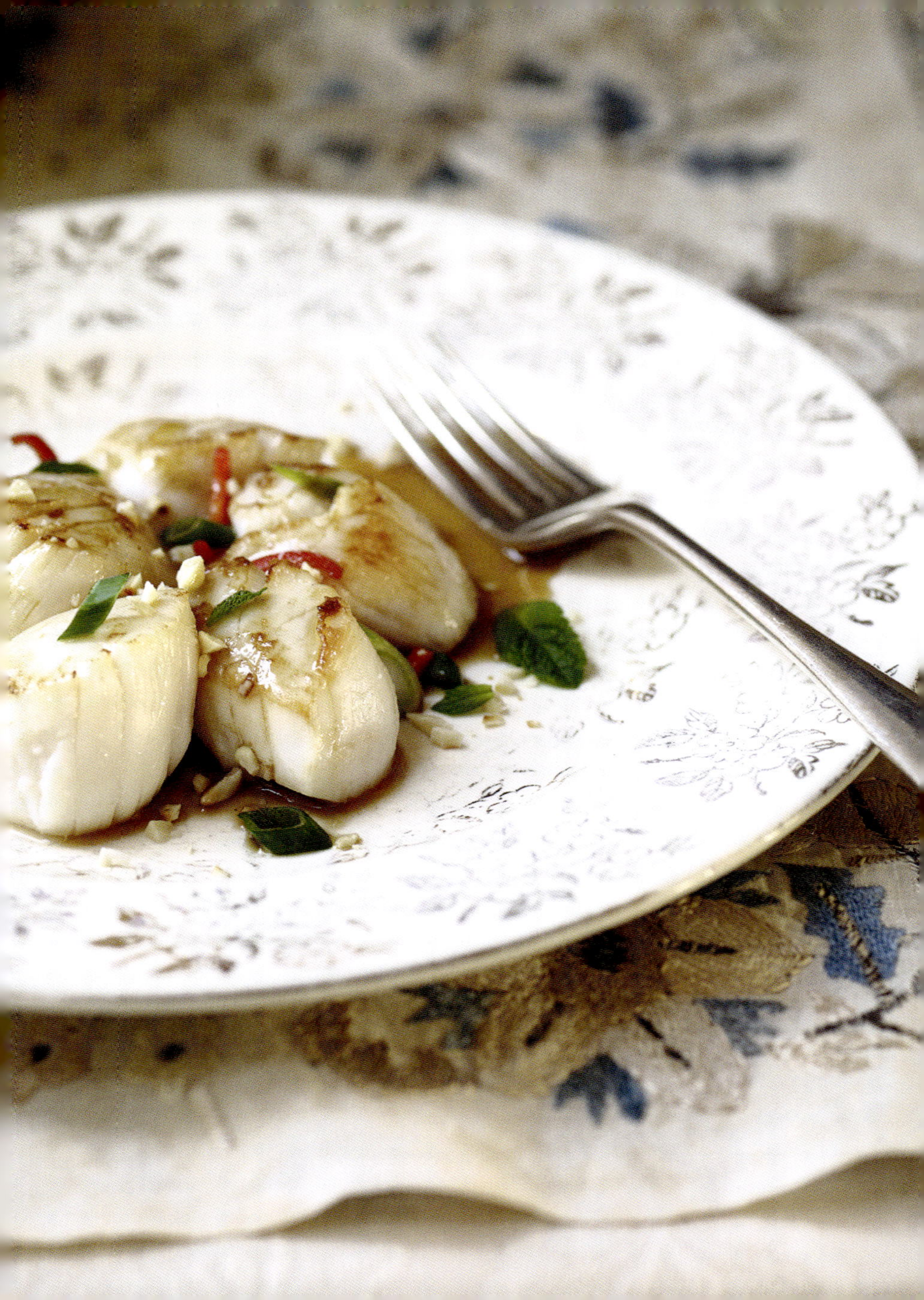

Garlic Mushrooms
ON TOASTED BRIOCHE

This classic French snack is given a quintessentially British touch with a spoonful of Fortnum's hot Tewkesbury Mustard. It makes an indulgent starter or light lunch, combining a mixture of mushroom varieties bathed in a creamy, tarragon sauce.

Serves 4

A knob of butter

1 tsp olive oil

300g mixed mushrooms, such as chestnut, oyster and enoki

1 garlic clove, sliced

2–3 tsp Fortnum & Mason Tewkesbury Mustard

125g crème fraîche

A little finely chopped fresh tarragon

4 slices brioche

8 slices cured ham, such as Bayonne

Salt and freshly ground black pepper

Watercress, to serve

Heat the butter in a large frying pan with the oil until the butter has melted. Swirl around the pan to cover. Add the mushrooms and sauté for 3-4 minutes, tossing every now and then until golden and cooked through. Add the garlic and cook for 1 minute.

Stir the mustard and crème fraîche together and add to the pan with the tarragon. Season well and continue to cook for 1-2 minutes until heated through.

Toast the brioche and divide among four plates. Spoon over the mushrooms, top with the ham slices and serve with a little watercress.

A Taste of the British Empire

If you were a major player in the British army during the 19th century, you were sure to be celebrated elsewhere. Colonel Skinner, who became Commander-in-Chief of British India, Major Grey, a Bengal Lancer's Officer and Brigadier Nicholson, famed for his role in quelling the Indian Mutiny in 1857, have been immortalised in the range of Fortnum's mango chutneys. The mild, subtle spice in Major Grey is enhanced by the light caramel tones of Demerara sugar. Taking it up a notch in spice and depth of flavour, the Colonel Skinner combines both red chillies and Scotch bonnet with Demerara and soft brown sugar. The most recent addition, created in 2006, Brigadier Nicholson, is bracing and punchy – just like the man himself, or so they say – whereby the lime and spice are let loose to weave their magic freely throughout the preserve alongside the rich taste of dark brown sugar.

Mustard Pastry Bites

These savoury treats are perfect as a canapé before dinner. Alternatively, they work equally well alongside the cheeseboard, with a selection of Fortnum & Mason chutneys.

Makes 14–16

60g butter, at room temperature

1 tsp Fortnum & Mason Piccadilly Wholegrain Mustard

25g Wensleydale cheese, grated

1 medium egg, beaten

70g plain flour

Sea salt, to sprinkle

Place the butter in a bowl and add the mustard, cheese and half the egg. Use a wooden spoon to work all the ingredients together to make a paste. Add the flour and continue to mix everything together to make a dough. Lay on a board, flatten into a disc, then wrap in clingfilm and chill for 30 minutes.

Preheat the oven to 180°C/350°F/gas mark 4. Unwrap the dough and roll it out to a thickness of about 0.5cm. Cut into 14–16 fingers.

Line a baking sheet with baking parchment and put the fingers on top, spaced well apart. Brush with the remaining egg and sprinkle with a little salt. Bake for 20–25 minutes until golden. Cool on a wire rack and store in an airtight container for up to three days.

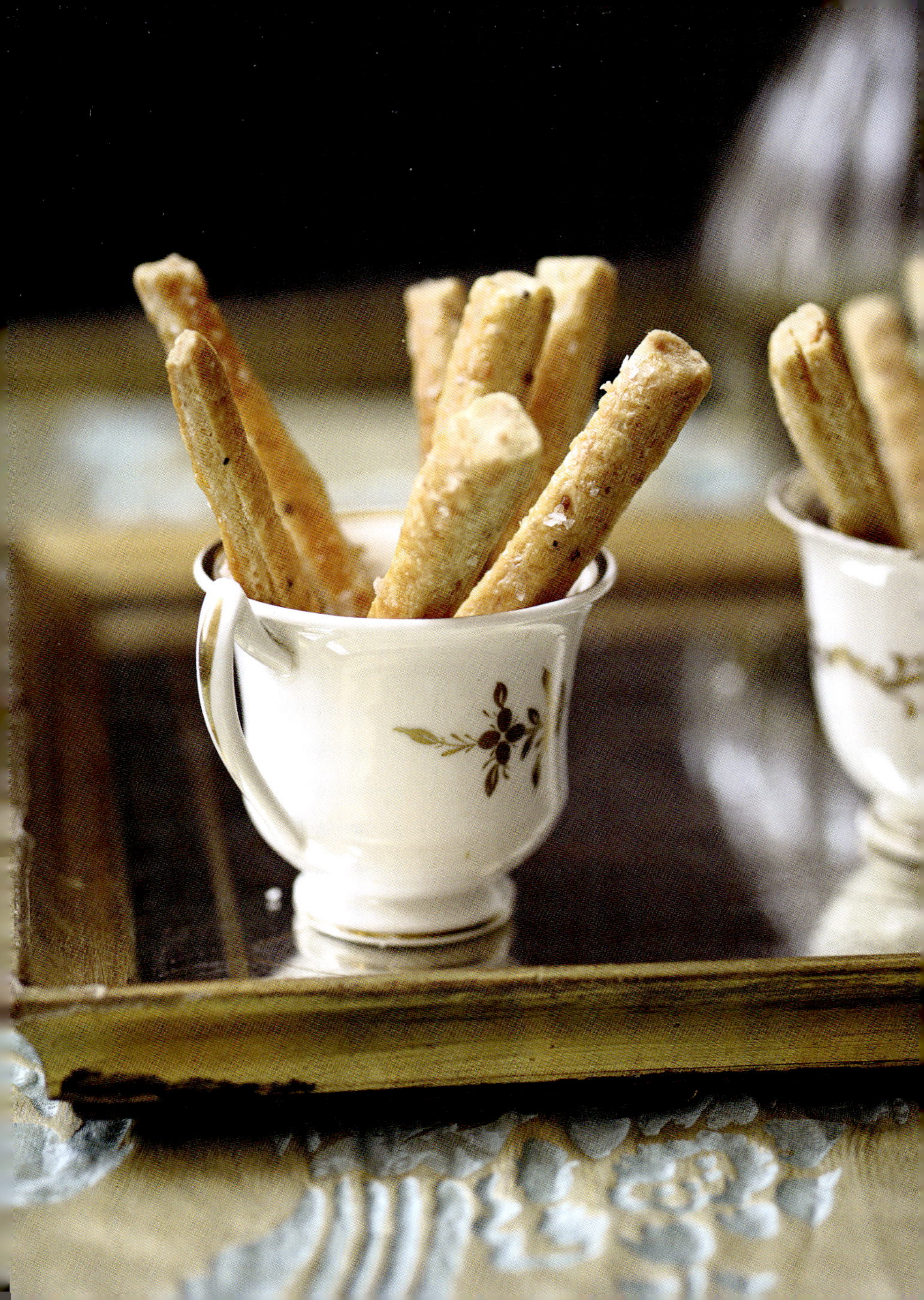

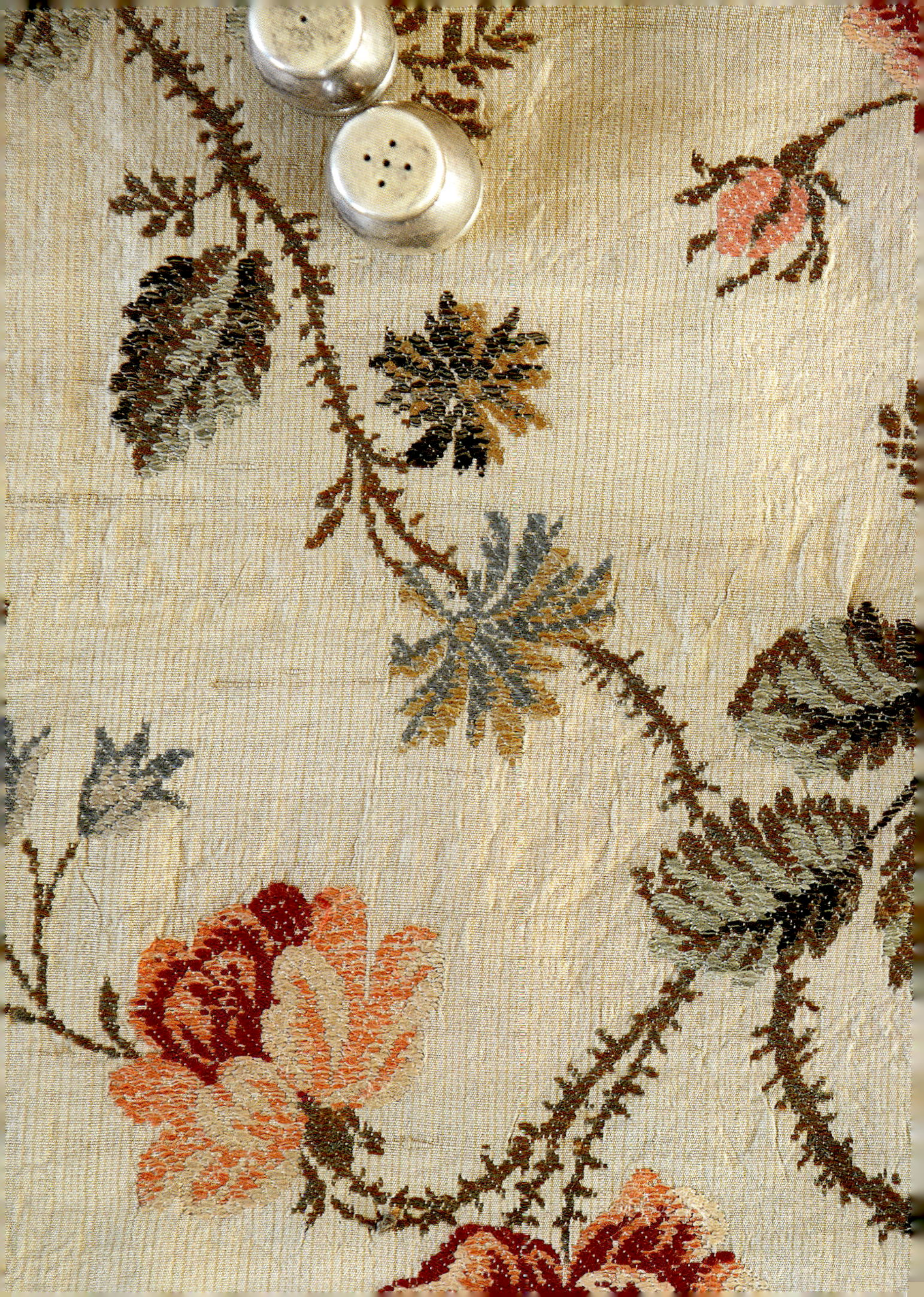

Main Courses

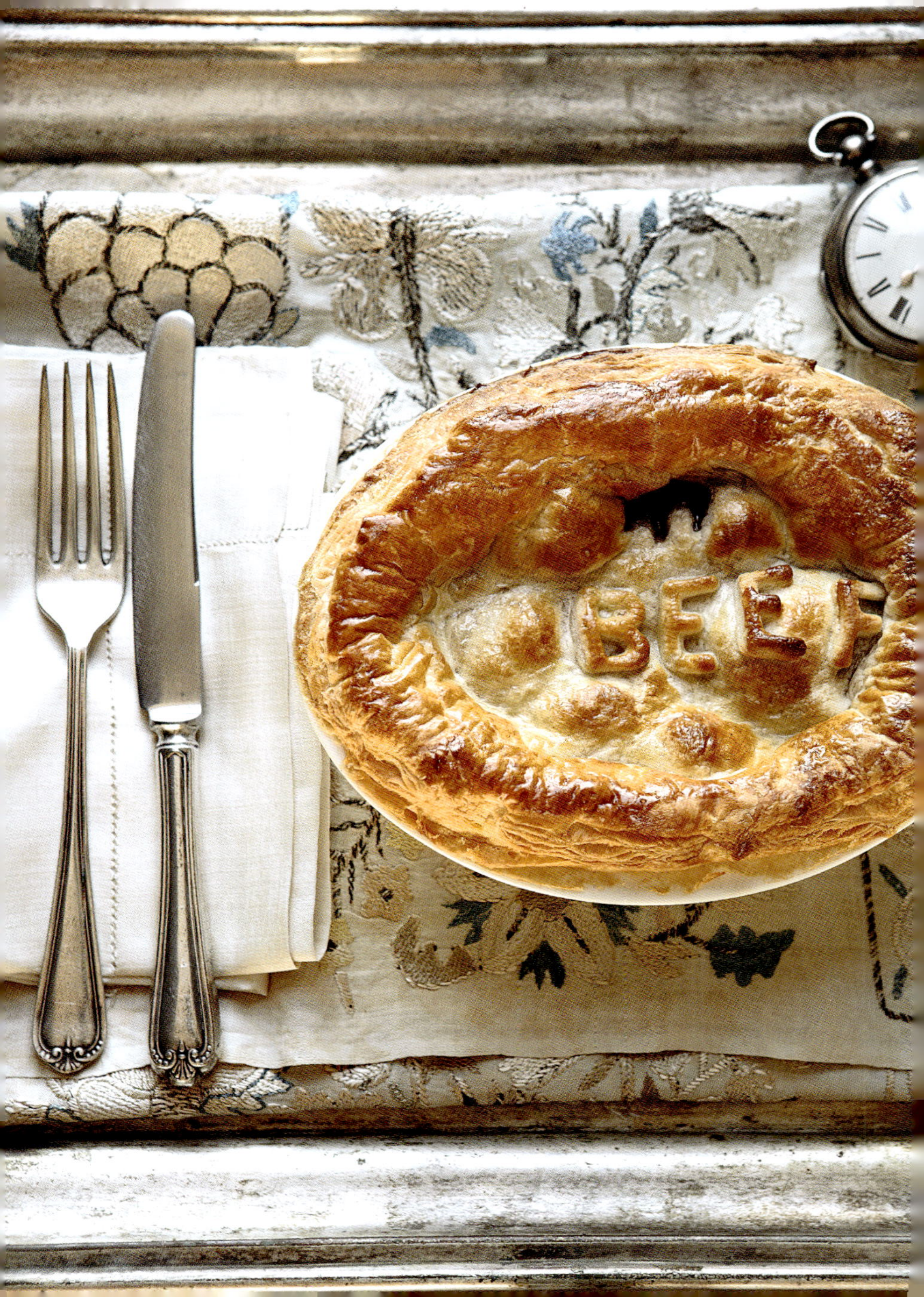
BEEF

Beef and Stout
PUFF PASTRY PIE

Cumberland Sauce is a classic partner to venison and duck but a spoonful works equally well stirred into this rich-bodied stew.

Serves 4

2 tbsp plain flour, plus extra for dusting

900g braising beef, cut into large chunks

2 tbsp sunflower oil

8 baby onions

4 carrots, peeled and cut into large chunks

2 celery sticks, cut into large chunks

300ml Guinness or other stout

600ml hot beef stock

1 tbsp Fortnum & Mason Cumberland Sauce

1 thyme sprig

1 bay leaf

500g pack all-butter puff pastry

1 medium egg, beaten

Salt and freshly ground black pepper

You will also need four 500ml pie dishes

Put the flour into a shallow dish and season well. Toss the beef in the flour, then heat 1 tablespoon oil in an ovenproof casserole pan and brown the beef in batches, taking care not to burn the juices. Remove the beef and set aside. Add the remaining oil and the vegetables, sauté for a few minutes, then remove from the pan and add to the beef.

Pour the stout into the pan and allow to bubble for 1–2 minutes, using a wooden spoon to scrape up all the sticky bits from the base. Return the beef and vegetables to the pan, then add the stock, Cumberland Sauce, thyme and bay leaf. Season well, cover with a lid and bring slowly to the boil. Reduce to a simmer and cook for 1½ hours until the beef is tender.

Preheat the oven to 200°C/400°F/gas mark 6. Roll out the pastry on a lightly floured board and use the pie dishes to cut out four lids. Use any remaining pastry to stamp out pastry to decorate.

Divide the beef stew among the pie dishes. Brush the rim of each pie dish with water and pop the lids on top, pressing them down lightly to stick. Brush any pastry decorations with water and arrange. Cut two little holes in the top of each pie then brush with beaten egg.

Bake the pies in the oven for around 30 minutes until the pastry is golden and puffed up. Serve immediately.

Spiced Roast Lamb
WITH FIGS AND HONEY

Marinating lamb in one of Fortnum's finest honeys and Indian spices gives it a wonderful mellow taste. The sauce is rich and flavoursome, so serve a simple accompaniment of just-boiled new potatoes and steamed green beans.

Serves 6

150g Fortnum & Mason runny honey

8 tbsp olive oil, plus extra to drizzle

4 tsp curry powder

Juice of 1 lemon

1.8kg leg of lamb

200g cherry tomatoes on the vine

6 figs, halved

Salt and freshly ground black pepper

In a large, sealable, non-metallic container, mix together the honey, olive oil, curry powder and lemon juice. Season well. Add the lamb and toss it in the marinade to coat completely. Cover, then put in the fridge to marinate for up to 24 hours.

Preheat the oven to 200°C/400°F/gas mark 6. Take the lamb out of the fridge and put it in a deep roasting tin along with any marinade, if remaining. Add 200ml cold water. Cover the entire tin with foil and seal tightly. Roast for 1 hour and 20 minutes or 20 minutes per 450g.

Around 20 minutes before the end of the lamb's cooking time, put the tomatoes and figs in a separate roasting tin, drizzle with oil and season. Remove the foil from the lamb at this point to allow the joint to brown. Cook the vegetables with the lamb for the remaining 20 minutes until tender.

When the lamb is cooked, transfer it to a warmed carving platter, cover with foil and allow to rest for 15 minutes. Spoon the fat off the juices in the pan and discard. Pour the juices into a warmed jug, adding any rested juices from the pan, and put the roasted tomatoes and figs into a serving dish. Carve the lamb and serve with the figs, tomatoes and sauce.

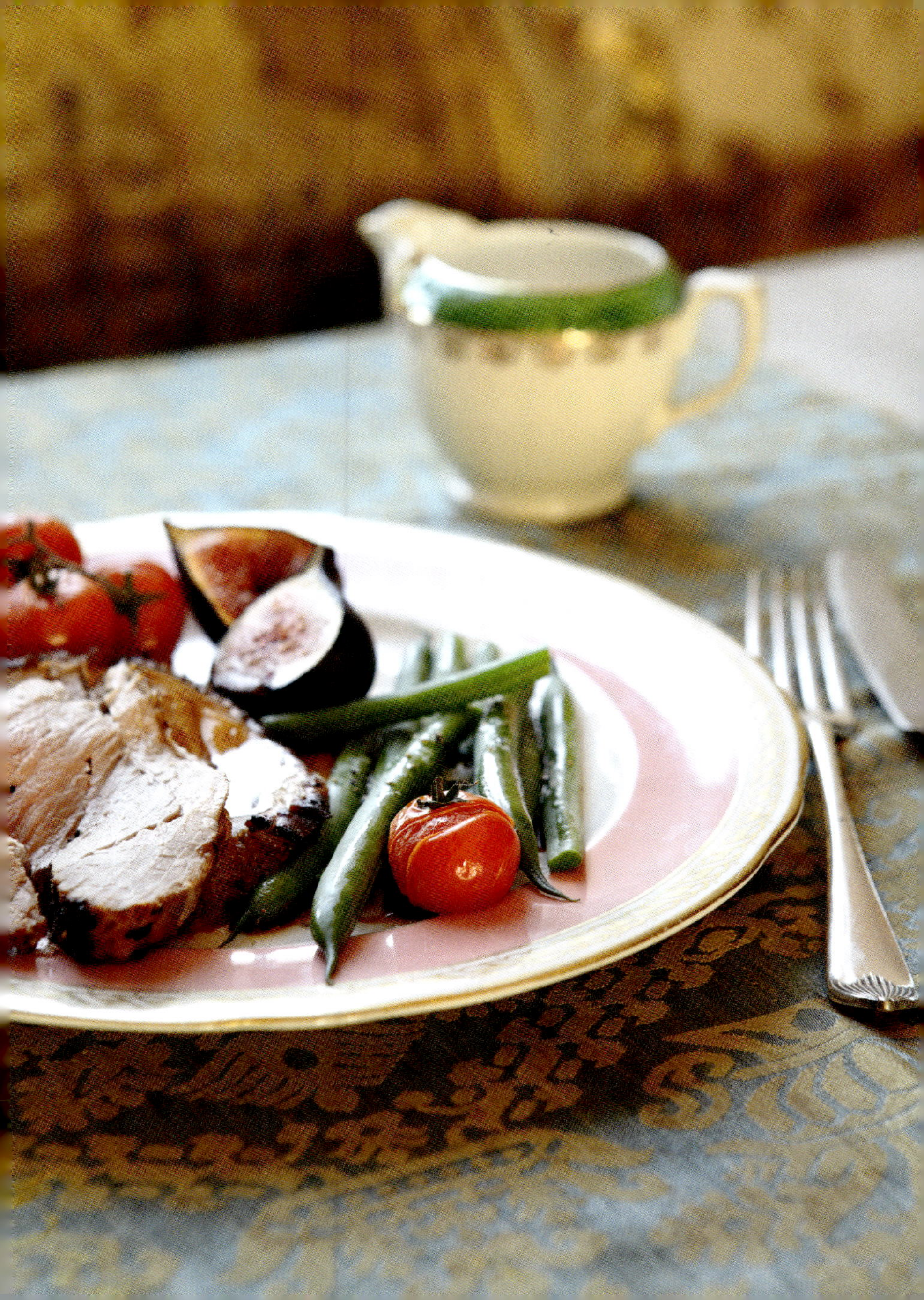

Marmalade-glazed HAM

Roast ham is a welcome treat whether it's cooked for a summer picnic, Boxing Day feast or a traditional Sunday lunch. This recipe calls for the joint to be finished with an orange and marmalade glaze, leaving it deliciously sweet on the outside and wonderfully moist on the inside. The stock can be used as a rich base for pea and ham or lentil soup.

Serves 6–8

1.2kg gammon joint

1 carrot and 1 celery stick, each cut into three pieces

1 onion, quartered

6 black peppercorns

1 bay leaf

1 thyme sprig

Juice of 1 orange

2–3 tbsp Fortnum & Mason Old English Hunt Marmalade No 2

Whole cloves

Salt and freshly ground black pepper

Put the gammon in a large pan and add enough cold water to cover. Add the carrot, celery, onion, peppercorns and herbs. Place a lid on the pan and bring gently to the boil. Skim any scum from the top and discard.

Turn down the heat and simmer gently for 1 hour 10 minutes or 25 minutes per 450g. Take the joint out of the pan and use a sharp knife to carefully remove the skin, leaving behind a thin layer of fat. Preheat the oven to 220°C/425°F/gas mark 7.

Mix together the orange juice and marmalade and season. Score the skin of the fat in a criss-cross pattern, then push a clove into each diamond shape. Put the joint in a small roasting tin and spoon over the marmalade mixture.

Roast in the oven for 15–20 minutes until the glaze is golden. Remove from the oven, cover with foil and allow the joint to rest for 10 minutes, then carve into slices to serve.

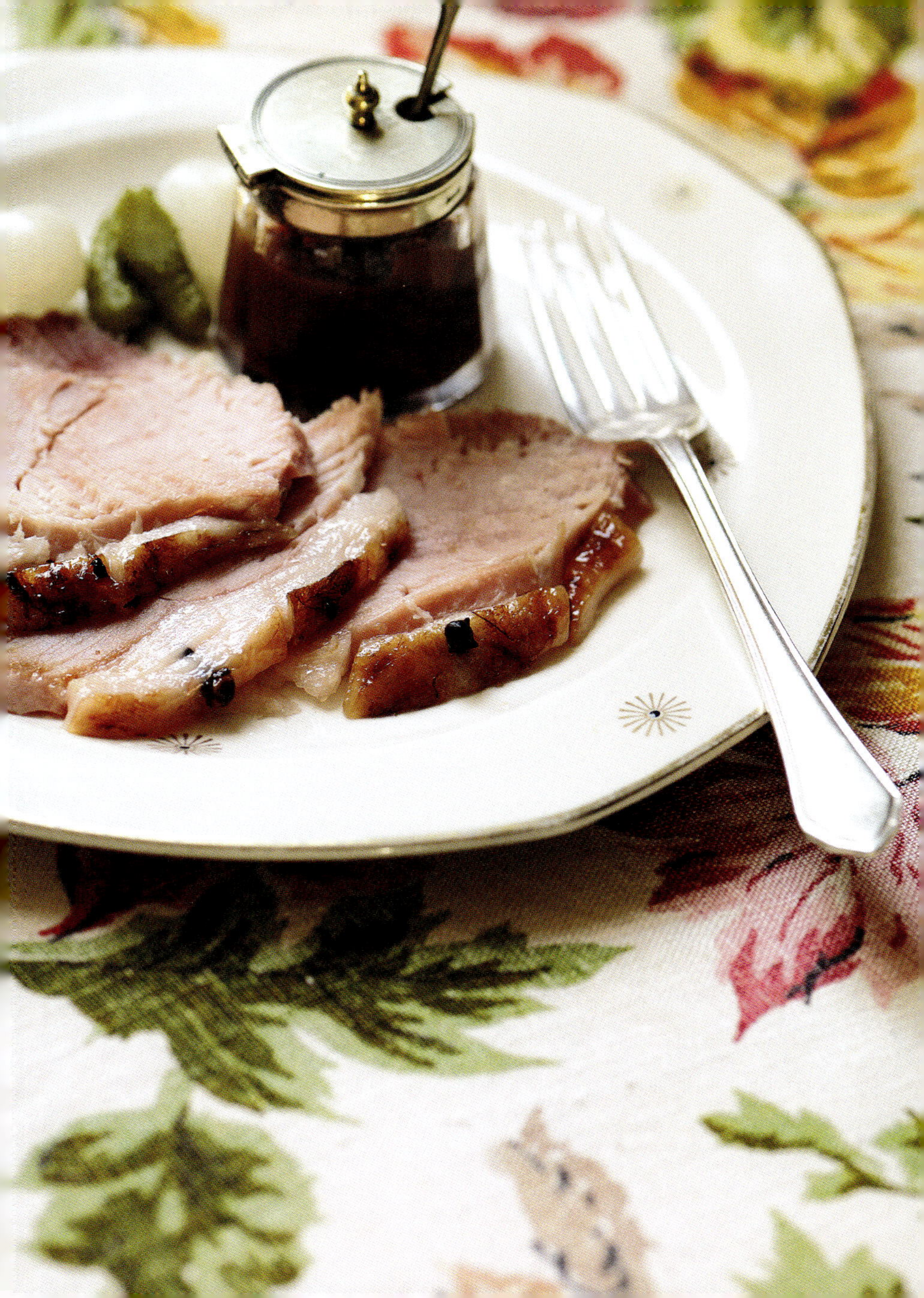

Pork Tenderloin
WITH PARMA HAM

This stunning dinner-party dish combines earthy mushrooms sweetened with Fortnum & Mason's magnificent Madeira Jelly and pork.

Serves 4

- A small knob of butter
- 1 tsp olive oil
- 1 shallot, finely chopped
- 200g chestnut mushrooms, finely chopped
- 1 tbsp Fortnum & Mason Madeira Jelly
- 1 tbsp brandy
- 600g pork fillet, trimmed
- 8 slices cured ham, such as Parma or Serrano
- 400g pappardelle pasta
- A little olive oil
- 100ml double cream
- 1 tbsp chopped flatleaf parsley, finely chopped
- Salt and freshly ground black pepper

Melt the butter with the oil in a pan. Add the shallot and cook until soft. Add the mushrooms, season then cover the pan and allow the mushrooms to cook for 4–5 minutes until softened and golden.

Stir in the Madeira Jelly and brandy and turn up the heat to cook off any juices. Spoon the mushrooms into a bowl and set aside to cool.

Preheat the oven to 200°C/400°F/gas mark 6. Lay the cured ham on a board, each piece overlapping, to measure the same length as the piece of pork. Spread the mushroom mixture over about two-thirds of the ham, leaving the top bare. Season well. Place the pork on top and bring the mushroom-covered part of the cured ham up and over the fillet, then fold over the top half of the ham to seal.

Lift the wrapped tenderloin into a roasting tin and pour in enough boiling water to cover the base by about 1cm. Roast in the oven for 40 minutes.

Cook the pasta until al dente. Drain, return to the pan and toss with a little oil and seasoning.

Lift the pork out of the tin, put on a warmed plate and cover. Set aside to rest for 10 minutes. Add the cream and 100ml boiling water to the tin. Season and place over a medium heat and cook for a few minutes to make a rich sauce. Pour any juices from the pork into the pan. Stir the sauce and parsley into the pasta. Divide among four plates, then slice the pork and serve on top of the pasta.

Duck Breasts
WITH PORT AND MORELLO CHERRY SAUCE

Stone fruit is a natural partner to the rich, savoury flavours of duck and here that sweet contrast is provided by Fortnum's Morello Cherry Preserve. Save the fat once the duck has been cooked and use it to roast potatoes until deliciously crisp.

Serves 6

- 6 duck breasts, skin on
- 1 tbsp Chinese five spice
- 2 tsp plain flour
- 200ml ruby port
- 500ml hot chicken stock
- 2 tbsp Fortnum & Mason Morello Cherry Preserve
- Salt and freshly ground black pepper
- Watercress, to serve

Preheat the oven to 200°C/400°F/gas mark 6. Lay the duck on a board and score the fat evenly three or four times. Rub the Chinese five spice all over the skin and season well.

Heat an ovenproof frying pan until hot and cook the duck, skin-side down, in batches until golden. Turn over and cook the other side for 2–3 minutes (If you don't have an ovenproof frying pan, transfer the duck to a roasting tin for this stage.) Roast in the oven for 15 minutes.

Place the duck on a warmed plate, cover and set aside to rest. Drain the excess fat from the pan and add the flour. Stir into the pan and cook for 1 minute.

Gradually add the port to the pan and keep stirring all the time to make a thick sauce. Add the stock next, seasoning as you go, with the preserve. Bring to the boil and simmer for around 5 minutes until saucy.

Add any juices from the duck to the sauce and stir in. Slice the duck and arrange on a plate. Spoon over the sauce and serve with the watercress.

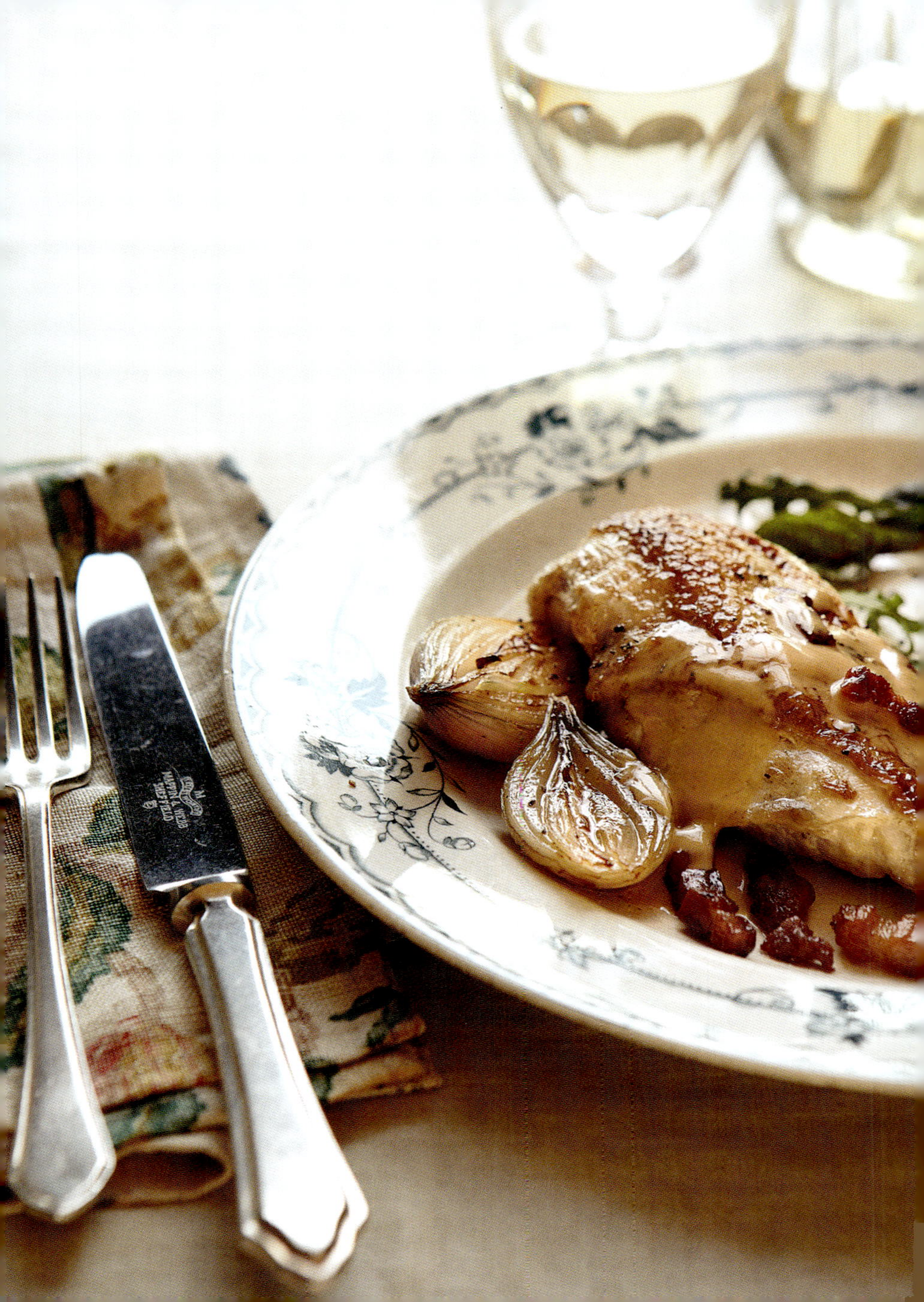

Honey Roast Chicken
WITH CARAMELISED SHALLOTS

Fragrant Fortnum's Scottish Heather Honey provides a subtle flavour and modern twist to this classic recipe. As the chicken breasts are gently braised in a rich stock-based sauce they take on a moist, melt-in-the-mouth texture.

Serves 4

A drizzle of olive oil

4 chicken breasts, skin on

A little butter

2 tsp plain flour

500ml hot chicken stock

2 tbsp Fortnum & Mason Scottish Heather Honey

6 banana shallots, halved

200g bacon lardons

4 tsp cider vinegar

Salad leaves, such as rocket and chard

Salt and freshly ground black pepper

Heat the oil in a large sauté or casserole pan and pan-fry the chicken breasts skin-side down until golden, then turn over and cook the other side. You will probably need to do this in two batches. Set aside on a plate.

Add a knob of butter to the juices left in the pan and stir in the flour. Cook on a gentle heat for 1 minute. Add the stock and bring to the boil. Return the chicken to the pan and season well. Cover and simmer for about 30 minutes until the juices from the chicken run clear.

Put another knob of butter in a large frying pan with the honey. Add the shallots, cut-side down, and cook for a couple of minutes over a medium heat until caramelised. Season well, add the lardons and continue to cook until golden. Stir in the cider vinegar and cook for 1 minute.

Divide the chicken among four plates. Spoon over the sauce from the pan, then arrange a handful of salad leaves on the side. Spoon over the caramelised shallot and lardon mixture with their juices.

Salmon
WITH A WARM CUCUMBER SAUCE

This sophisticated creamy sauce made from mustard, lemon and Fortnum's honey adds fresh and zesty flavours to a simple pan-fried salmon dish. Serve with buttered Jersey Royals and freshly steamed asparagus to complement the summery flavours. The sauce would also work very well with pan-fried monkfish.

Serves 4

- 4 x 150g fillets lightly smoked fresh salmon
- 1 tbsp olive oil
- ½ cucumber, peeled, seeded and thinly sliced
- 1 tbsp Dijon mustard
- 1 tbsp Fortnum & Mason Salisbury Plain Honey
- Juice of ½ lemon
- 100ml double cream
- Salt and freshly ground black pepper

Place a dry non-stick frying pan over a medium heat until hot. Season the salmon and fry, skin-side down, for about 5 minutes until half the flesh has turned opaque. Turn over on the other side and continue to cook until the other side is opaque and the salmon is just pink in the middle.

While the salmon is cooking, heat the oil in a pan and add the cucumber, mustard and honey. Shake the pan to mix all the ingredients together. Season well.

Add the lemon juice and stir in, then add the cream. Stir everything together to make a sauce and cook on a low heat for a couple of minutes to allow it to thicken.

Place the salmon on four warmed plates, then spoon the sauce over each fillet.

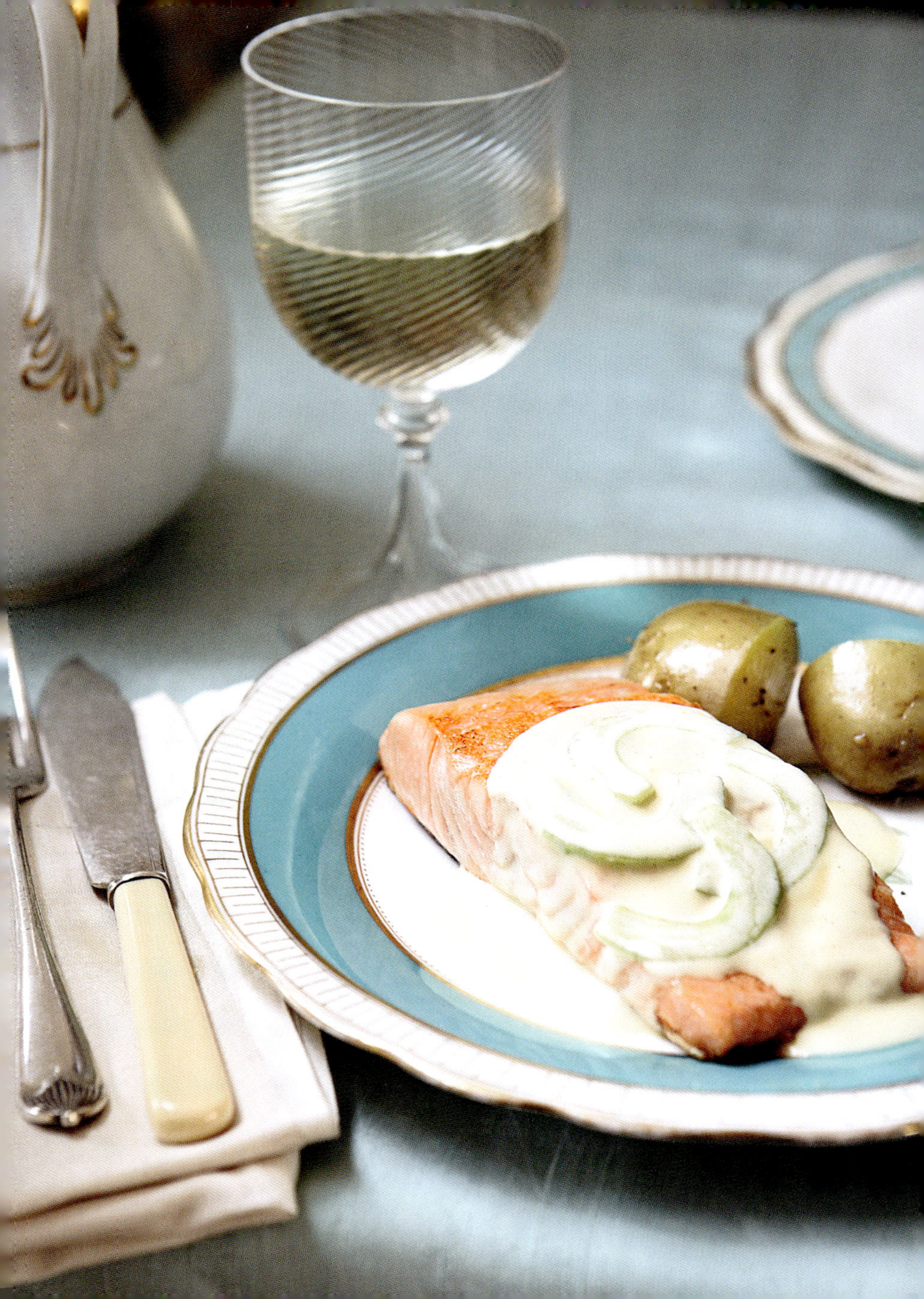

WARM NEW POTATO AND
Spinach Salad

A new, lighter take on the traditional potato and mayonnaise salad. This recipe combines the sweetness of Fortnum's Shropshire Honey Mustard with creamy crème fraîche. Add the spinach with the dressing to allow it to wilt down perfectly in the heat of the pan.

Serves 4–6

800g new potatoes, halved if large

1 shallot, finely diced

2 tsp white wine vinegar

1 tbsp Fortnum & Mason Shropshire Honey Mustard

100g crème fraîche

2 handfuls of baby leaf spinach

Salt and freshly ground black pepper

Put the potatoes in a large pan of salted water, cover, bring to the boil and simmer for 12–15 minutes until tender.

Meanwhile, put the shallot in a small bowl with the vinegar and add a pinch of salt. Set aside.

Drain the potatoes well and return to the pan. Mix together the shallot and vinegar with the mustard and crème fraîche. Add to the pan with the spinach. Season well. Replace the lid and shake the pan. This will help to wilt the spinach and coat the potatoes in the dressing. Serve immediately.

Carrots with Honey, ORANGE AND SESAME

Small and chunky Chantenay carrots are the best variety for cooking with this moreish glaze. Delicious Fortnum's honey enhances their sweetness while toasted sesame seeds add bite to their tender texture.

Serves 6

600g Chantenay carrots

A pinch of salt

Juice of 1 orange

1 tbsp Fortnum & Mason runny honey

1 tsp sesame seeds, toasted

Salt and freshly ground black pepper

Put the carrots in a pan and cover with cold water. Add the salt. Cover, bring to the boil and simmer until tender. Drain well and return to the pan.

Whisk together the orange juice, honey and sesame seeds and season well.

Add the dressing to the warm pan and heat very gently over a low heat to allow the carrots to infuse with the flavours of the dressing.

Main Courses

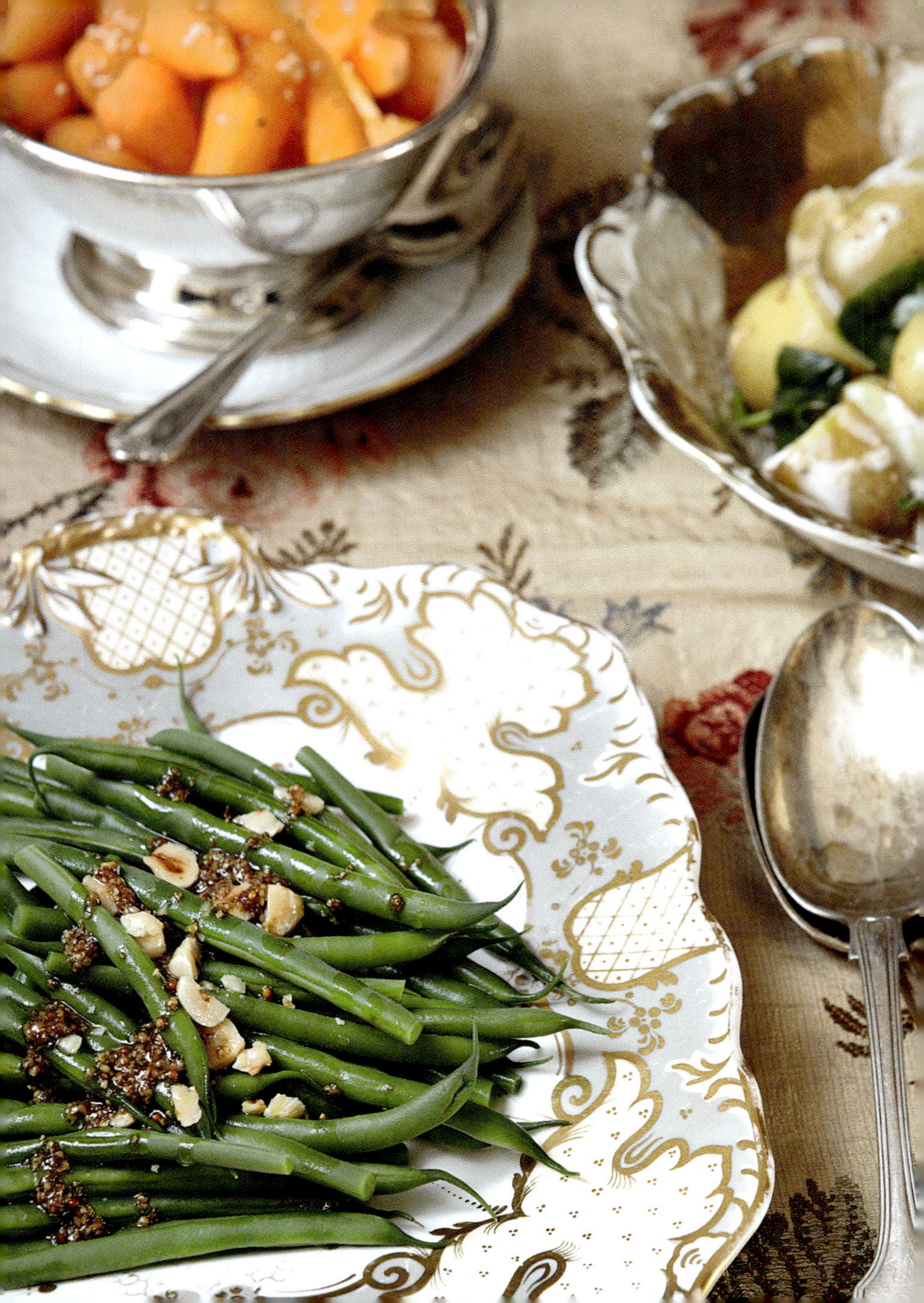

French Beans
WITH MUSTARD AND HAZELNUT DRESSING

This splendid vegetable side combines French beans tossed with hazelnuts to create a dish with extra bite. Cook the beans until just tender to create myriad textures and coat with a punchy dressing made with Fortnum's mustard.

Serves 6

500g French beans, trimmed

1 tsp Fortnum & Mason Piccadilly Wholegrain Mustard

2 tbsp extra virgin olive oil

1 tsp balsamic vinegar

15g hazelnuts, toasted and chopped

Salt and freshly ground black pepper

Put the beans in a pan and cover with cold water. Add the salt. Cover, bring to the boil and simmer for 3–4 minutes until tender. Drain well and return to the pan.

Whisk together the mustard, olive oil, balsamic vinegar and hazelnuts and season well. Place the beans onto a serving plate and spoon the dressing evenly over the vegetables to coat.

MONTGOMERY'S CHEDDAR AND
Onion Tart

Serves 8

For the pastry

200g plain flour, plus extra for dusting

100g butter, chopped and chilled

For the filling

40g butter

1 tsp olive oil

3 large onions, finely sliced

3 medium eggs

75g crème fraîche

150ml double cream

Jar of Fortnum & Mason Florentine Fruit & Nut Chutney

100g Montgomery's Cheddar, grated

Salt and freshly ground black pepper

Whiz the flour and butter in a food processor until the mixture resembles breadcrumbs. With the machine running, add 3–4 tablespoons of iced water and pulse until thick and crumbly. Tip into a bowl, bring together with your hands and knead lightly. Wrap in clingfilm and chill for 15 minutes.

Roll out the pastry on a lightly floured board and line a deep 20cm fluted tin. Prick the base all over, cover with clingfilm and chill for 15 minutes.

Melt the butter with the oil in a large pan. Stir in the onions and season. Cover with a piece of wetted, scrunched up greaseproof paper. Cover with a lid. The wet greaseproof creates steam in the pan and helps to cook the onions. Turn the heat down low and cook, stirring until softened, for 1 hour.

Preheat the oven to 200°C/400°F/gas mark 6. Bake the pastry case blind (using baking beans) for 15–20 minutes until the pastry is dry to the touch. Cool.

Beat the eggs, then brush a little over the base of the pastry. Return to the oven for 2 minutes. Reduce the oven temperature to 150°C/300°F/gas mark 2.

Whisk the remaining eggs in a bowl with the crème fraîche and cream. Season well. Spread a couple of tablespoons of chutney over the pastry case. Drain the onions and spread on top. Pour over the egg mixture then top with the grated cheese. Bake for 40–50 minutes until the filling is set. Cool a little then remove from the tin and serve with a green salad.

TWICE-BAKED LANCASHIRE *Cheese Soufflé*

A brilliant prepare-ahead dinner-party dish. Cook the soufflés first, then reheat them with just a drizzle of cream, so they are wonderfully light in texture and richly flavoured. White pepper is preferable to black in this dish, as it blends into the mixture more easily.

Serves 6

50g butter, plus extra for greasing

275ml milk

A slice of onion

Leaves from two fresh thyme sprigs, plus extra leaves to garnish

125g Lancashire cheese

40g plain flour

3 medium eggs, separated

6 tbsp double cream

Salt and ground white pepper

To serve

Fortnum & Mason Piccadilly Piccalilli

Green salad

You will also need six 100ml ramekins

Butter the ramekins well. Preheat the oven to 180°C/350°/gas mark 4. Bring the milk to a boil in a small pan with the onion and thyme, then turn off the heat and set aside. Roughly chop the cheese.

Melt the butter in a pan over a low heat and stir in the flour. Cook for 1 minute. Discard the onion from the milk, then very slowly over a low heat, pour in the milk and stir well to ensure there are no lumps. Cook for 1-2 minutes to thicken the sauce then stir in the cheese and the egg yolks and season.

Whisk the egg whites in a grease-free bowl until stiff peaks form. Add a large spoonful of whites to the cheese sauce and fold in to loosen the mixture, then fold the remaining egg whites into the sauce.

Place the ramekins into a roasting tin, then divide the mixture evenly among them. Pour boiling water halfway up the sides of the dishes and bake for 15 minutes. Remove from the water and cool. Cover and chill for up to a day until ready to cook.

When ready to cook, run a table knife around the edge of each ramekin to loosen the soufflé and turn each out into a small heatproof bowl. Preheat the oven to 220°C/425°F/gas mark 7. Spoon 1 tablespoon cream over each soufflé. Season with salt. Bake in the oven for 10 minutes then serve immediately with Fortnum's Piccalilli and a salad.

Main Courses

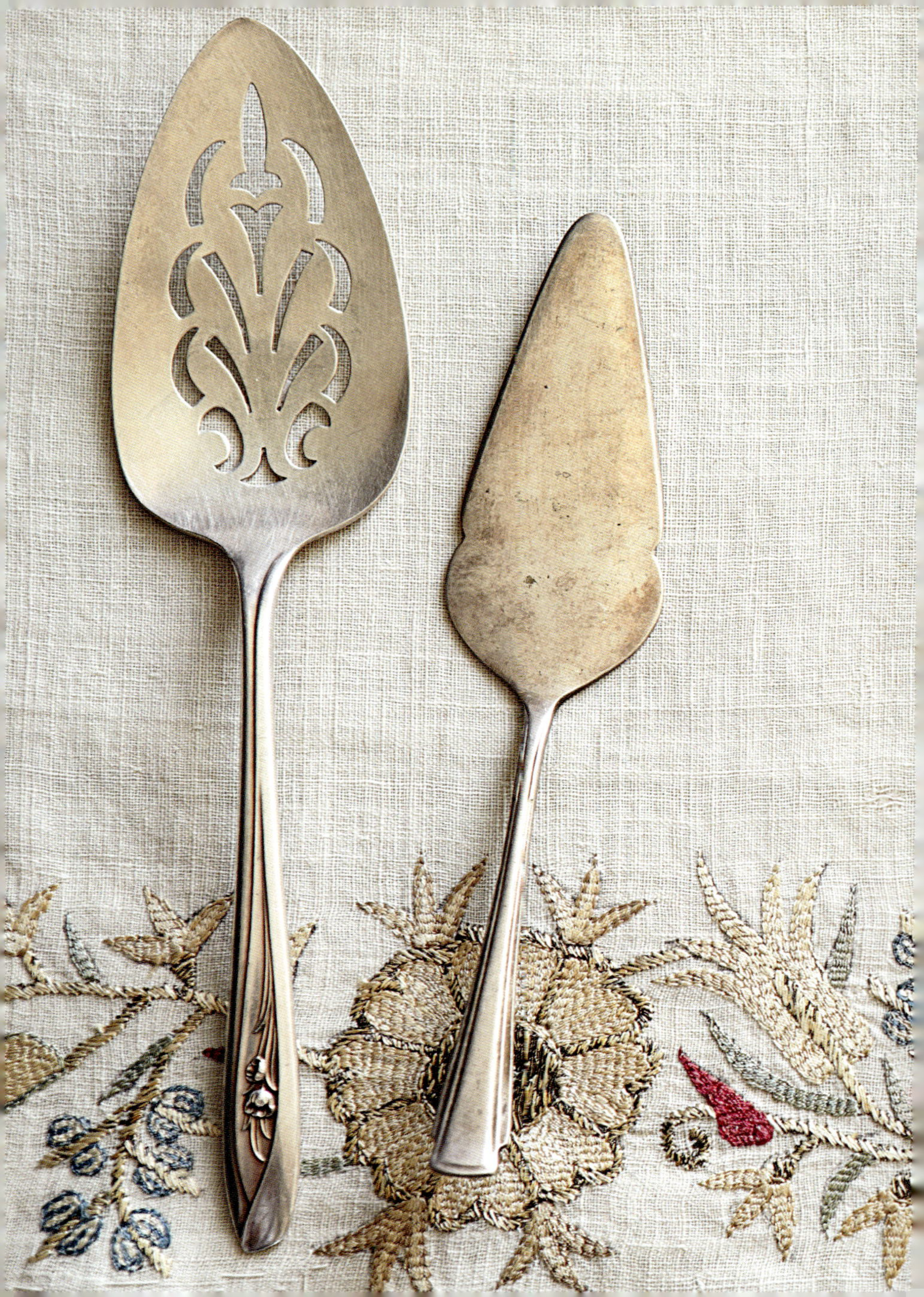

Puddings

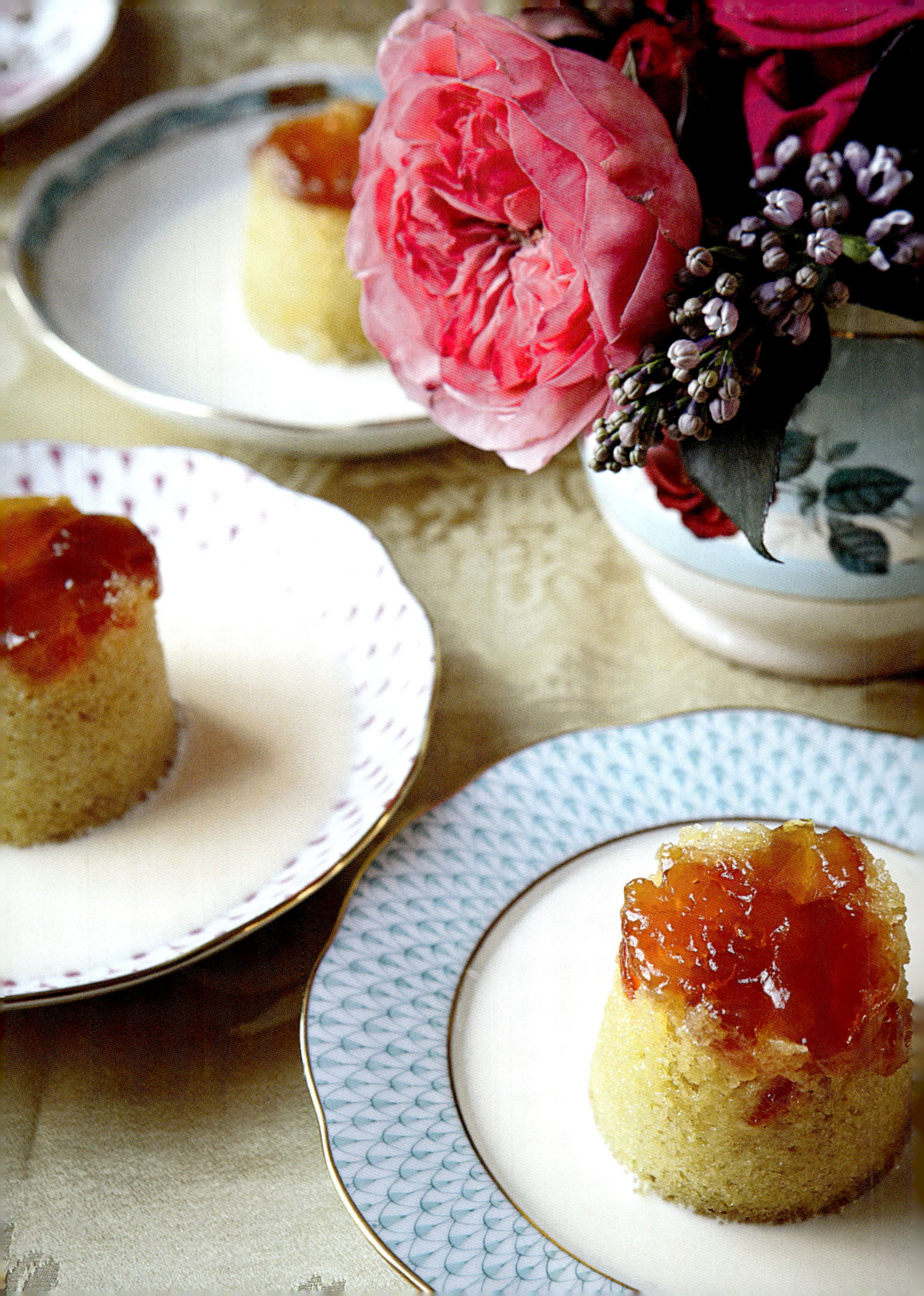

Marmalade Puddings
WITH WHISKY CUSTARD

These irresistible puddings are crowned with one of Fortnum's best marmalades and have a moreish feather-light texture, that comes from the steaming. Serve with the fresh custard, which is laced with a splash of whisky.

Serves 6

100g softened butter, plus extra for greasing

4–6 tbsp Fortnum & Mason Orange Marmalade with Fortnum's Whisky

Juice of ½ orange

100g golden caster sugar

2 medium eggs, beaten

100g self-raising flour

Zest of 1 orange

For the whisky custard

300ml double cream

2 large egg yolks

1–2 tbsp whisky

2 tbsp golden icing sugar

You will also need six 110ml dariole moulds

Preheat the oven to 200°C/400°F/gas mark 6. Butter the dariole moulds and line the bases with baking parchment. Cut out six rounds of parchment to fit inside each mould and six pieces of foil to fit over the top of the moulds.

Gently heat the marmalade and orange juice together then divide among the moulds.

Beat the butter and sugar in a bowl until soft and creamy. Gradually add the beaten egg, adding a little flour if it looks like the mixture might curdle. Fold in the orange zest and remaining flour.

Divide this mixture among the moulds and lightly place a parchment round on top of each. Wrap each mould in foil, securing it at the top.

Put the puddings in a roasting tin and pour in enough boiling water to come half way up the sides of the puddings. Cook in the oven for 35 minutes.

Make the custard. Heat the cream in a small pan until bubbles appear round the outside. Beat the egg yolks, whisky and icing sugar in a bowl. Pour the scalded cream onto the egg yolks and whisk well. Return the mixture to the pan and heat gently, stirring, until the custard thickens slightly.

Remove the foil and parchment from the moulds and turn each pudding out onto a shallow bowl, removing the parchment on the base. Pour the custard around the side and serve immediately.

Timeless Traditions

Keen sportsmen are fully aware of the benefits of a jolly good breakfast prior to an event. Huntsmen and the shooting party of the Pytchley Hunt, one of the oldest recorded gatherings in England, stand testament to that. Their energy-fuelled feast includes slices of hot buttered toast with Fortnum's Old English Hunt Marmalade (named after the event) and consists of a medium-cut peel and raw soft brown sugar.

For those who prefer a palate-tingling experience, our Burlington Breakfast marmalade is made with a finer sliced peel and raw cane sugar. The result? It makes for a unique kick-start to the day with a light, bright and fresh taste.

CHOCOLATE AND *Prune Cake*

Chocolate and prune is a winning combination as demonstrated in this delicious recipe where the cocoa-rich flavour is heightened by the dark-tasting preserved fruit. This sweet treat which is half cake, half pudding is best served warm, fresh from the oven, with a spoonful of melting clotted cream alongside it.

Serves 8–10

100g ready-to-eat prunes

100ml brewed tea, such as Fortnum & Mason Earl Grey Tea

200g dark chocolate (at least 50% cocoa solids), broken into pieces

100g butter, chopped

4 medium eggs

50g golden caster sugar

50g Fortnum & Mason English Salisbury Plain Honey

50g plain flour, sifted

Preheat the oven to 180°C/350°F/gas mark 4. Grease and flour a 20cm loose-bottomed cake tin.

Put the prunes and the tea in a small pan and bring to the boil. Simmer until soft. Put in a food processor or blender and whiz to make a purée.

Melt the chocolate and butter together in a heatproof bowl set over a pan of simmering water, making sure the base doesn't touch the water. Stir gently together and set aside to cool.

Whisk the eggs, sugar and honey together in a bowl until thick and moussey. Carefully fold in the chocolate mixture, prune purée and flour. Spoon into the tin and bake for 25 minutes.

Cool in the tin for 5 minutes, resting on a wire rack. Remove the cake from the tin, using a palette knife to slip underneath it and transfer it to a board. Slice into pieces and serve while still warm.

Pear Tart
WITH APRICOT GLAZE

Serves 8

For the pastry
175g plain flour,
1 tbsp golden icing sugar
75g cold butter, diced
1 egg yolk

For the filling
3 pears, peeled
300ml white wine
1 strip of lemon peel
1 bay leaf
150g caster sugar
100g softened butter
1 large egg, beaten
1 tbsp plain flour
100g ground almonds
Juice of 1 lemon
1½ tbsp Fortnum & Mason Apricot Preserve, No. 98
Crème fraîche, to serve

You will also need a 12 x 36cm tranche tin

Put the pears in a small pan with the wine, lemon peel, bay leaf and 50g sugar. Cover with greaseproof paper and a lid. Gently bring to the boil, then reduce to a simmer and cook for 15 minutes, until just tender. Cool, reserving the liquid, then carefully halve the pears, scooping out each calyx and core.

For the pastry, whiz the flour, icing sugar and butter in a food processor until the mixture looks like breadcrumbs. Mix the egg yolk with 1 tablespoon cold water. Add to the mixture. Pulse until crumbly. Tip into a bowl, bring it together with your hands, wrap in clingfilm and chill for 15 minutes. Preheat the oven to 200°C/400°F/gas mark 6.

Roll out the pastry on a lightly floured board and use to line the tranche tin. Cover and chill for 10 minutes. Prick the base, cover with greaseproof paper and fill with baking beans. Blind bake for 12 minutes until the surface is almost dry. Lift out the paper and beans and return the case to the oven for a few minutes until the pastry is dry to the touch.

Reduce the oven to 180°C/350°F/gas mark 4. Beat the butter and remaining 100g sugar until soft and creamy. Gradually add the egg, then fold in the flour and ground almonds. Spread all over the pastry base, then put the pears on top. Bake for 20–25 minutes until golden. If the top looks as if it is browning too much, cover loosely with foil.

Boil the reserved wine mixture until the liquid measures about 50ml then stir in the preserve. Take the tart out of the oven, brush the jam mix over the top and cool. Slice and serve with crème fraîche.

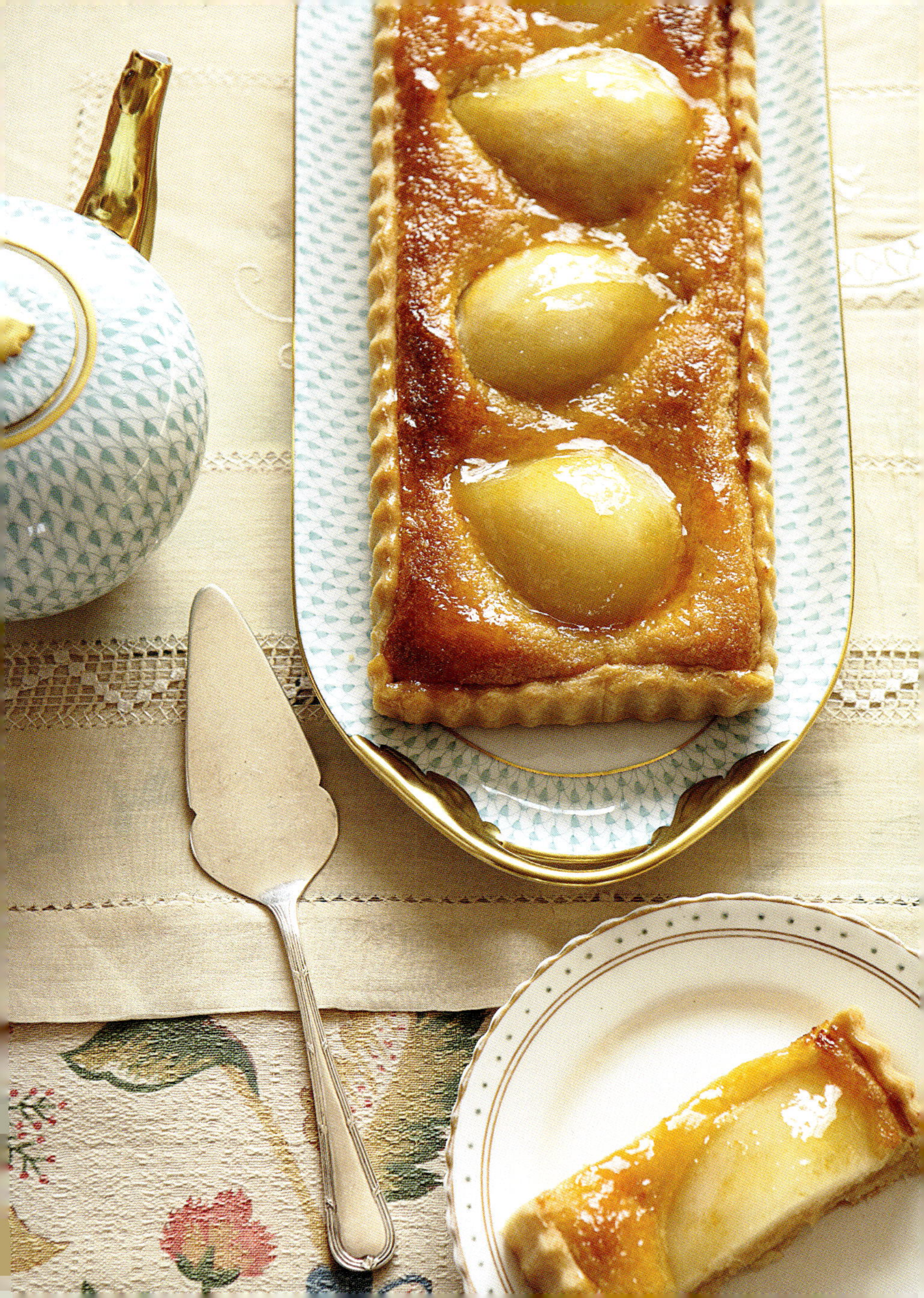

Apple and Walnut Strudel Tart

This fruit-filled tart, which uses the core ingredients of a strudel, combines crumbly, butter-rich pastry and a crisp filo top. Chopped apple, walnuts and spice, mixed together with Fortnum & Mason's delicious Bramble Jelly with Cider, makes a sumptuous filling between these two layers. Serve with a drizzle of single cream.

Serves 8–10

For the pastry

190g plain flour

2 tbsp icing sugar, plus extra for dusting

95g butter

1 egg yolk

For the filling

550g dessert apples, such as Gala

75g walnuts, chopped

35g raisins

½ tsp ground cinnamon

3 tbsp Fortnum & Mason Bramble Jelly with Cider

130g filo pastry (around 7 sheets)

50g butter, melted

Put the flour and icing sugar in a food processor and add the butter. Whiz the ingredients together until the mixture resembles breadcrumbs. Mix the egg yolk with 1–2 tablespoons cold water. Pulse again until the mixture starts to clump together. Tip into a bowl and bring together with your hands, kneading gently. Wrap in clingfilm and chill for 15 minutes.

Roll out the pastry and use to line a deep 20.5cm loose-bottomed tart tin. Cover and chill for 15 minutes. Preheat the oven to 200°C/400°F/gas mark 6. Prick the base of the pastry all over with a fork, cover with greaseproof paper, then fill with baking beans. Bake for 15 minutes, remove the greaseproof paper and beans then return to the oven and cook for a few minutes until it feels dry to the touch. Set aside.

Peel and finely dice the apples. Put in a bowl with the walnuts, raisins and ground cinnamon. Melt the bramble jelly in a small pan, then stir it into the apple mixture. Toss everything together to mix well.

Spoon the apple mixture into the pastry case. Put each sheet of filo pastry on top of the apples, scrunching it up as you go. Drizzle over the melted butter to cover, then bake in the oven for 30 minutes. Cool a little before removing from the tin. Dust with icing sugar, then slice and serve.

Honey CRÈME CARAMEL

This classic creamy pudding takes on a new flavour with the addition of Fortnum & Mason's English Salisbury Plain Honey, with its buttery flavours. It's a delicious pudding that is simple to make, just watch the caramel as it cooks – it should bubble until dark brown. It shouldn't be too dark that the resulting sauce tastes bitter, nor should it be too light otherwise the pudding will not have the rich depth of flavour.

Serves 6

For the caramel

20g Fortnum & Mason English Salisbury Plain Honey

80g caster sugar

For the pudding

4 eggs

45g Fortnum & Mason English Salisbury Plain Honey

500ml full-fat milk

Preheat the oven to 150°C/300°F/gas mark 3. Make the caramel by putting the honey, sugar and 1 tablespoon water into a heavy-based pan. Heat gently to dissolve the sugar. Bring up to the boil and cook until the mixture is bubbling and dark brown – it should smell very rich. Pour into a 1-litre ovenproof dish, tipping it around so it covers the base. Leave to cool.

Meanwhile, make the pudding. Put the eggs and honey into a bowl and stir together with a wooden spoon. Pour the milk into a pan and bring just to the boil. Take off the heat and add a splash to the egg mixture. Stir in, then gradd the remaining milk, stirring all the time. Strain into a jug then pour into the dish containing the caramel.

Put the dish in a roasting tin and pour boiling water halfway up the sides of the dish. Cook in the oven for 50 minutes to 1 hour until the pudding is set on top.

Remove from the tin and allow to cool until just warm. Turn out onto a plate and serve immediately.

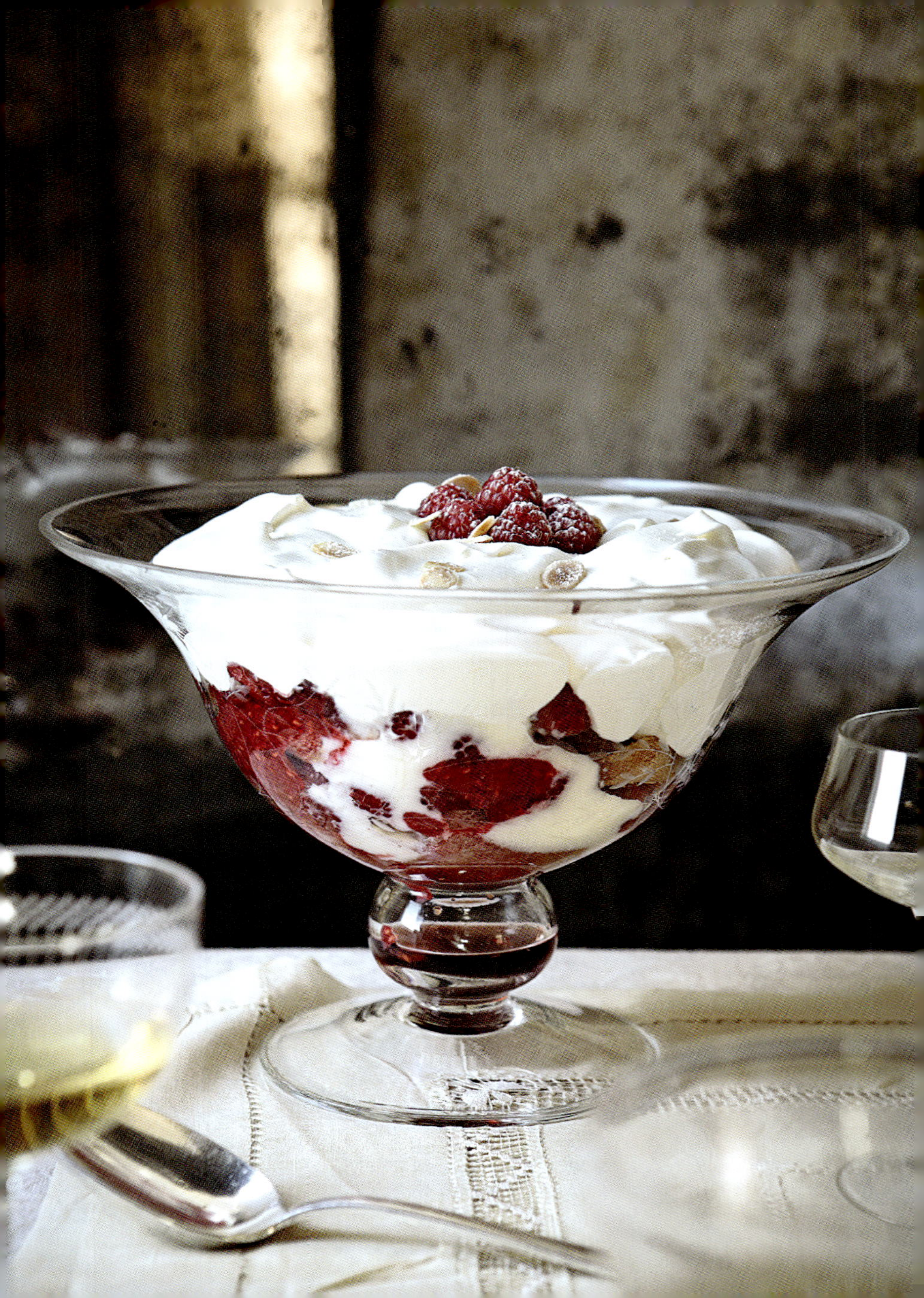

SCOTTISH *Raspberry Trifle*

A classic celebratory British pudding which dates back to the 1600s when it consisted of little more than spiced, sweetened cream. It developed in the middle of the 18th century to use the combination of ingredients we know today. This recipe is a decadent confection of fresh raspberries, sponge cake sweetened with a boozy fruit liqueur, homemade custard and clouds of whipped cream. Take care when whipping the cream so it doesn't end up too stiff – it should be softly peaking when you finish whisking.

Serves 6–8

- 2 egg yolks
- 1 tbsp cornflour
- 50g golden caster sugar
- 1 tbsp vanilla extract
- 600ml full-fat milk
- 500g raspberries
- 12 trifle sponges
- Around 5 tbsp Fortnum & Mason Raspberry Seedless Preserve, No.93
- 4–5 tbsp Chambord raspberry liqueur
- 600ml double cream
- Icing sugar
- 25g flaked almonds, toasted

Make the custard. Mix together the egg yolks, cornflour, sugar and vanilla extract. Pour the milk into a pan and bring to the boil. Turn off the heat. Pour a little onto the egg mixture and stir in, then add the remaining milk and stir to mix everything together. Rinse the pan.

Return the mixture to the pan and heat gently, stirring all the time until the mixture coats the back of the spoon. Pour into a container and cover loosely with a piece of clingfilm, then cool.

Put 200g of the raspberries in a food blender and whiz to make a purée. Cut each trifle sponge in half lengthways then spread the cut side of each half with the jam. Sandwich each sponge back together. Set aside a handful of raspberries for decoration, then layer the remainder in a bowl with the trifle sponges and purée, drizzling over a little liqueur at each layer.

Spoon over the custard. Whip the cream in a bowl with 1 teaspoon icing sugar until thick, but still soft. Spoon the cream over the top of the custard. Decorate with the remaining raspberries and the flaked almonds and dust with icing sugar.

Lemon and Lime CHEESECAKE

A delicious homemade shortcake base sits beneath this citrus-rich dessert. The cheesecake needs to be made a day ahead to give it time to chill and set, then taken out of the fridge half an hour before serving to allow it to come to room temperature and for the flavours to develop.

Serves 12

For the base

75g soft butter

40g granulated sugar

150g plain flour

For the filling

500g cream cheese

125g unrefined granulated sugar

1 heaped tbsp cornflour

3 medium eggs

150ml double cream

4 tbsp lemon and lime curd (see recipe, page 118)

Zest each of 1 lemon and lime

To decorate

100g golden caster sugar

1 each lemon and lime, finely sliced

Preheat the oven to 200°C/400°F/gas mark 6. First, make the base. Beat the butter and sugar together in a bowl. Stir in the flour and continue to mix until the mixture looks crumbly. Transfer to a 20cm springform cake tin and use the back of a spoon to press the mixture evenly into the tin until it looks paste-like. Chill for 15 minutes.

Bake the base in the oven for 15 minutes. Set aside to cool. Reduce the oven temperature to 150°C/300°F/gas mark 3.

Whisk the cream cheese, sugar, cornflour and eggs together in a bowl. Add the double cream and whisk in, then fold in the curd with the lemon and lime zest.

Spoon into the tin and bake for around 1 hour until just set in the middle. Remove from the oven and place on a wire rack to cool completely. Cover and chill overnight.

To decorate, put the sugar in a pan with 100ml water. Add the lemon and lime slices and place over a medium heat. Simmer for around 5 minutes until the slices are cooked. Carefully lift them out of the pan and set aside. Reduce the syrup to around 50ml, then cool.

Arrange the lemon and lime slices on top of the cheesecake, then serve sliced with a little syrup.

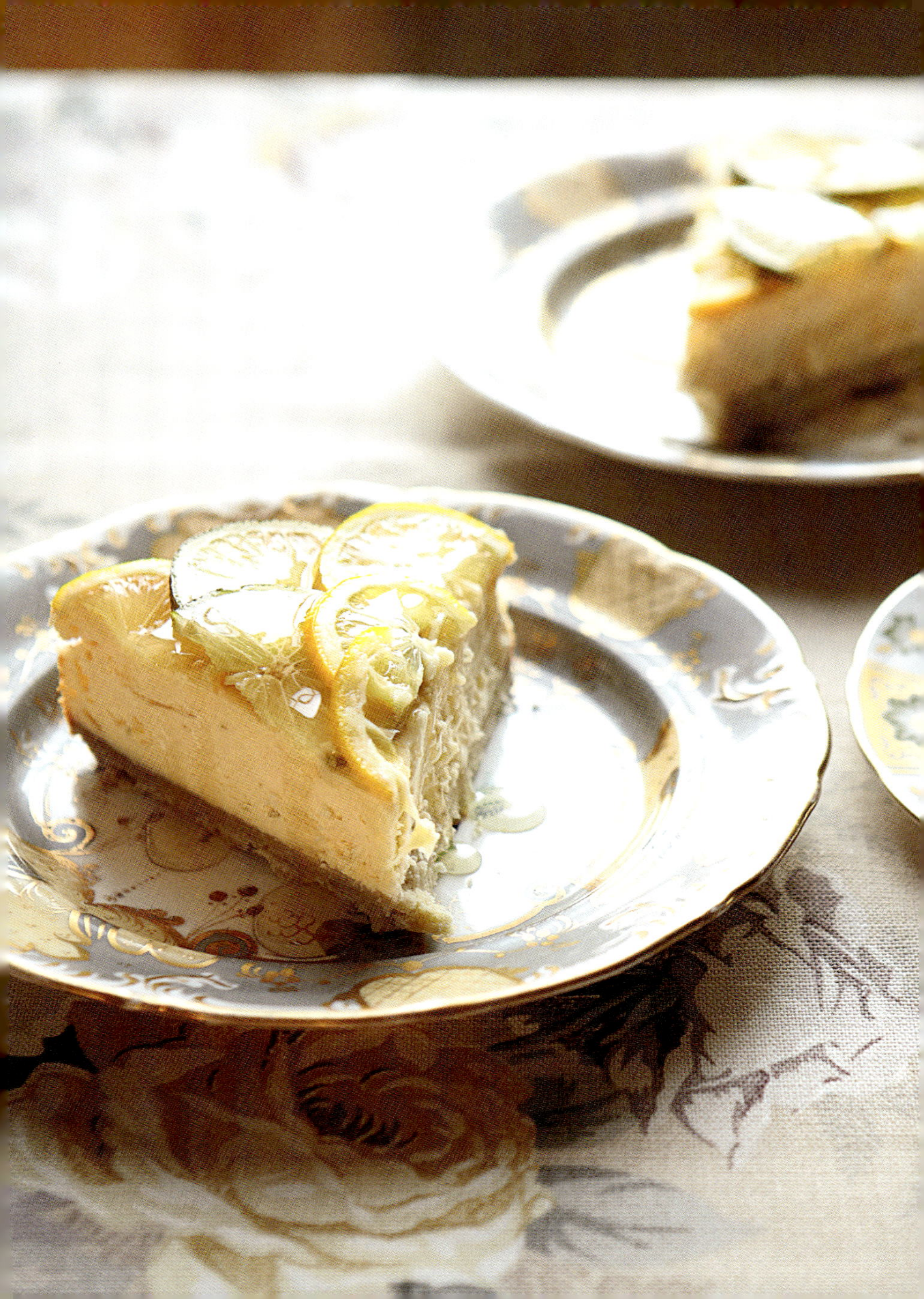

Lavender Ice Cream

This fragrant ice cream uses one of Fortnum's most interesting honeys, made from lavender grown on Mont Ventoux in Provence. It is irresistible on its own, garnished with crystallised lavender, or served with a fruit tart. It will store in the freezer for up to one month.

Serves 6

200ml double cream

400ml single cream

6 lavender flower heads

75g Fortnum & Mason French Lavender Honey

4 egg yolks

Pour the double and single cream into a pan. Add the flower heads and bring just to the boil. Turn off the heat and set aside to infuse for 15 minutes.

Put the honey and egg yolks in a bowl and stir together with a wooden spoon. Strain the infused cream into the bowl and stir all the ingredients together. Rinse the pan.

Return the mixture to the pan and heat gently, stirring all the time, to make a custard. It's ready when the mixture coats the back of the spoon. Strain the mixture into a clean bowl. Cool quickly by placing it over another bowl filled with ice and cold water.

Pour into a freezeable container and place in the freezer. Stir the ice crystals back into the mixture every two to three hours until frozen solid. Alternatively, use an ice-cream machine to churn until firm then freeze.

Poached Peaches

Fresh peaches are one of summer's best offerings. Delicately scented and full of flavour, they're delicious fresh but also wonderful cooked. Try them in this recipe using Fortnum's Ginger Preserve, which adds a subtle spicy kick to the syrup.

Serves 6

6 peaches, not too ripe

350ml white wine

1 tbsp Fortnum & Mason Ginger Preserve, No.73

125g caster sugar

1 lemon

Put the peaches in a large pan. Add the wine, ginger preserve and caster sugar. Use a vegetable peeler to remove four strips of peel from the lemon, taking care not to remove any white pith, and add them to the pan. Cover with a sheet of greaseproof paper and put a lid on the pan. Bring gently to the boil, then reduce the heat to its lowest point and simmer for around 15 minutes until the peaches are tender.

Carefully lift the peaches out of the pan and peel away and discard the skin. Put in a bowl, pour over the syrup and cool a little. These are best served lukewarm.

Puddings

Prosecco Jelly
WITH SUMMER FRUITS

This light delicate dessert is the perfect refreshing ending to lunch or dinner on a warm summer's day.

Serves 6

75g each raspberries, blueberries and strawberries

5 gelatine leaves

75cl bottle Fortnum & Mason Prosecco

100g Fortnum & Mason English Salisbury Plain Honey

Divide the summer fruits among six champagne saucers or flutes. Soak the gelatine in a small bowl of cold water.

Pour the Prosecco into a pan and add the honey. Heat gently, stirring to dissolve the honey, then gently bring to the boil and simmer for 2–3 minutes. Remove from the heat.

Lift the gelatine out of the bowl and add to the warm Prosecco mixture. Stir to dissolve the gelatine, then pour into a jug and divide among the glasses. Chill for at least 4 hours until set.

Take out of the fridge about 20 minutes before serving the jelly to allow to come to room temperature.

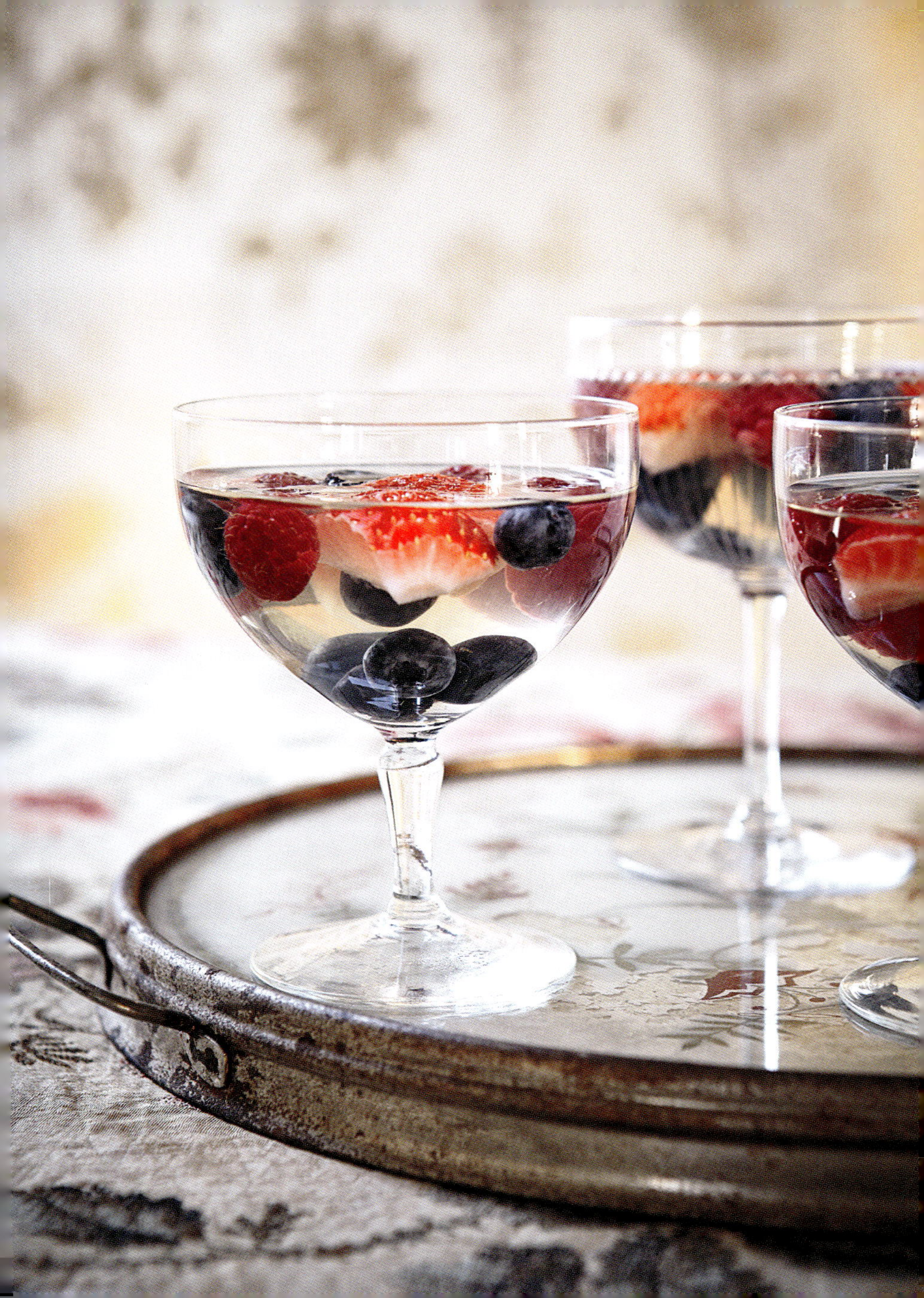

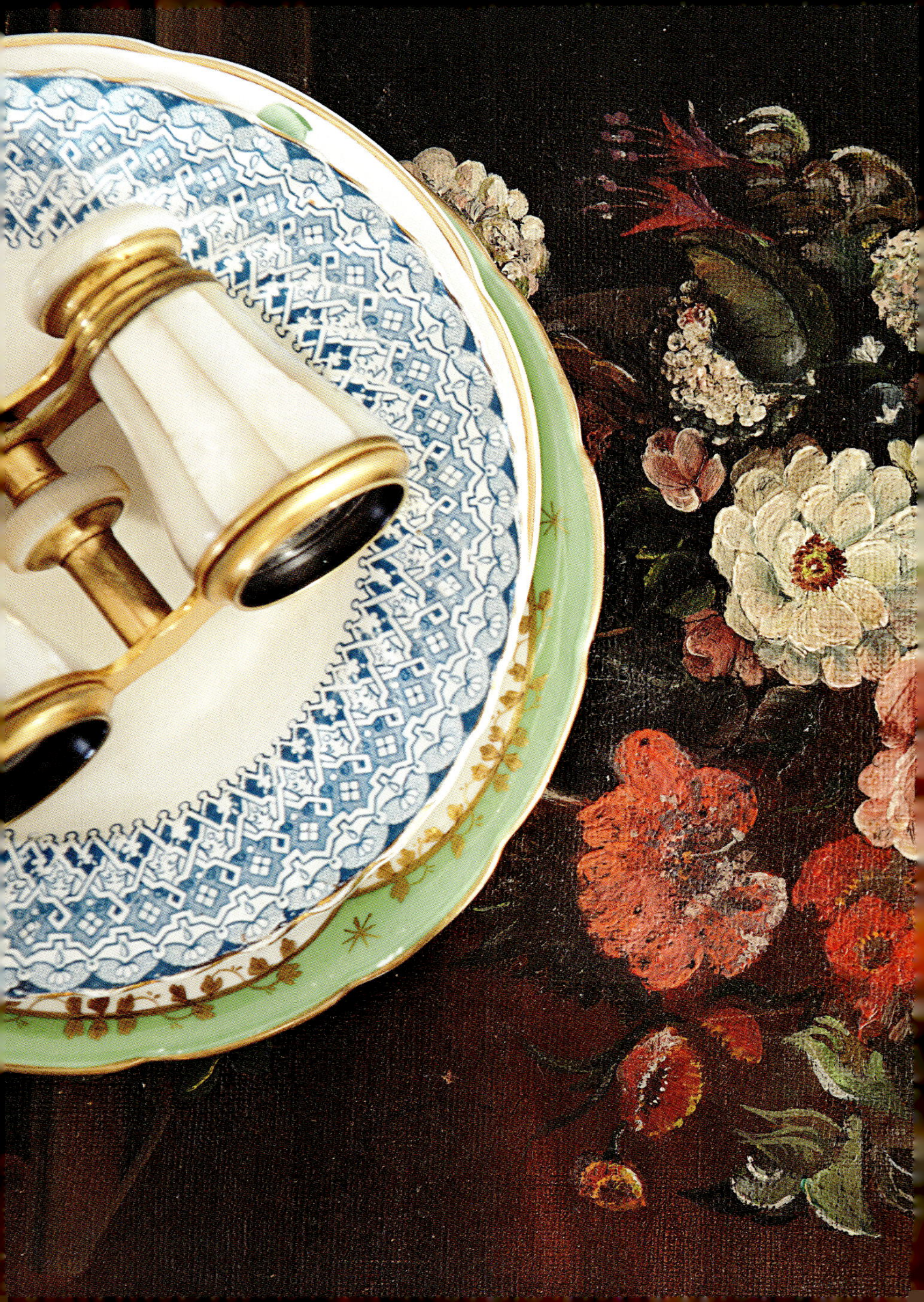

Bakes

Granary and Rye ROLLS

Warm freshly baked rolls straight from the oven are a delight whether they're enjoyed with butter and jam for breakfast or with a warming bowl of soup for lunch. These have a hearty texture, thanks to the rye flour, but also a deliciously soft crumb.

Makes 8 rolls

15g fresh yeast or 7g dried

300–350ml milk

1 tsp Fortnum & Mason runny honey

350g granary flour

150g rye flour, plus extra for shaping

1½ tsp salt

A little sunflower oil

Put the yeast in a bowl. If using fresh yeast, crumble it in. Heat the milk until lukewarm, then pour over the yeast and add the honey. Stir together to dissolve the yeast.

Sift the flours into a bowl, adding any bits left in the sieve, then stir in the salt. Make a well in the centre of the flour and pour in the yeast mixture. Use a knife to mix everything to make a dough then knead on a board until soft and smooth. If you're using a freestanding mixer, use the dough hook for this stage.

Put the dough in a clean, lightly oiled bowl and cover. Allow to rise in a warm place for about 1 hour until doubled in size. Take the dough out of the bowl and knead it very lightly on a floured board. Shape it into a round and flatten it slightly.

Line a baking sheet with baking parchment. Slide the flattened dough onto it, then set aside in a warm place for about 1 hour to prove until the dough springs back when lightly touched.

Preheat the oven to 200°C/400°F/gas mark 6. Cut the dough almost in half, then across horizontally, then divide each quarter into two to make eight wedges. Bake for 30–35 minutes until golden, or until the rolls sound hollow when tapped on the base. Slide onto a wire rack and cool, then store in an airtight container and enjoy within three days.

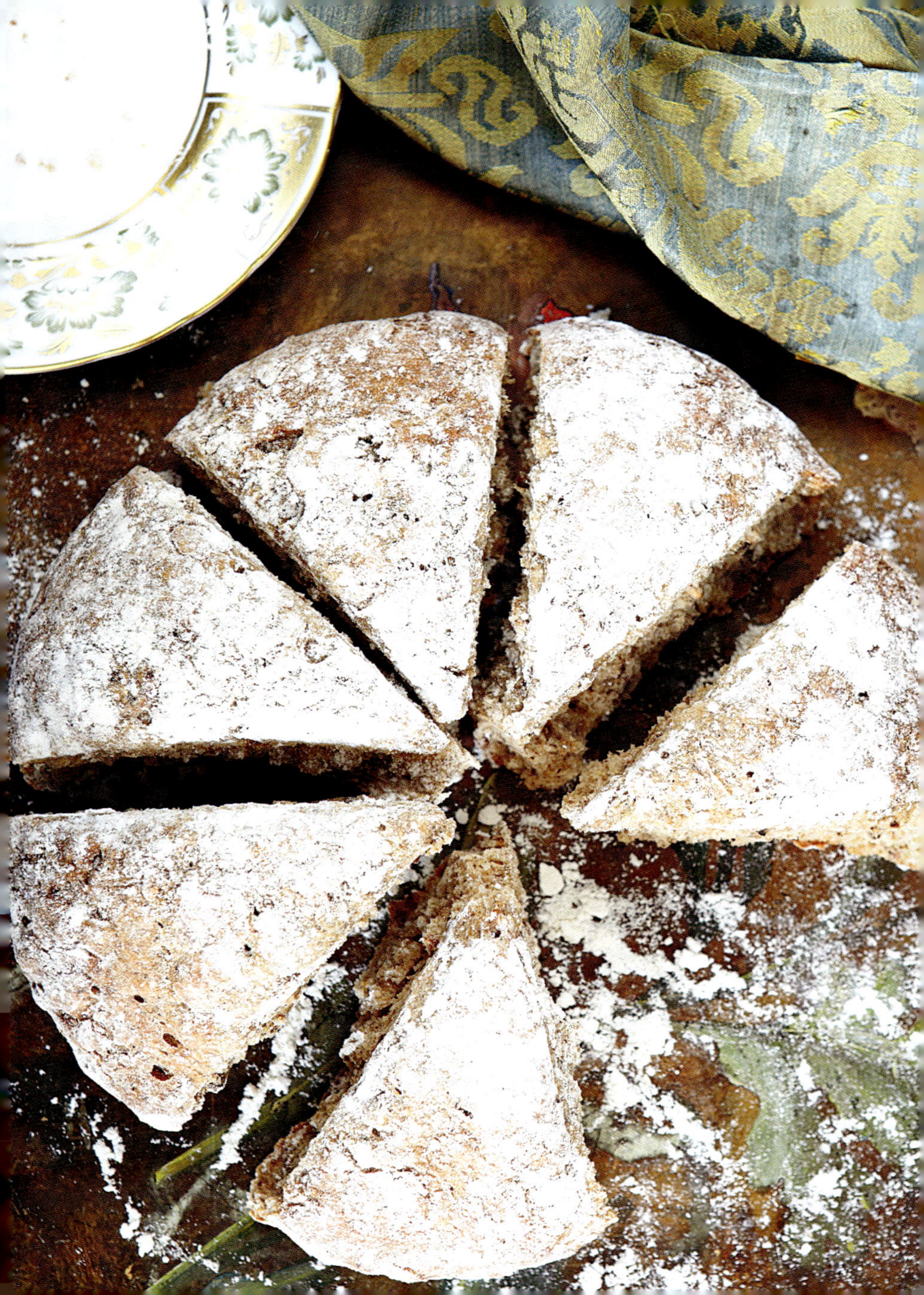

Seeded Soda Bread

This quick-to-make-and-bake loaf can be ready within an hour and is delicious with cream cheese or slices of smoked salmon. Use only the lightest of touches when bringing all the ingredients together into a dough, otherwise it will have a heavy texture.

Makes 1 loaf
250g plain flour
225g wholemeal flour
1 tsp bicarbonate of soda
1 tsp salt
2 tbsp sesame seeds
2 tbsp pumpkin seeds
2 tbsp sunflower seeds
284ml carton of buttermilk
75ml milk

Preheat the oven to 220°C/425°F/gas mark 7. Sift the flours into a large bowl. Reserve the bits from the wholemeal left in the sieve and set aside in a bowl. Stir in the bicarbonate of soda, salt and seeds.

In a separate bowl, mix together the buttermilk and milk. Make a well in the centre of the dry ingredients and pour in the buttermilk. Mix with a knife until the ingredients come together, then very lightly knead on a board for 1-2 minutes to make a soft dough. Shape it into a flat round and sprinkle the remaining bits in the sieve on top.

Use the handle of a wooden spoon to make a cross in the middle. Slide onto a baking sheet lined with baking parchment and bake for 10 minutes, then reduce the oven temperature to 200°C/400°F/gas mark 6. Continue to bake for around 25 minutes until it sounds hollow when tapped underneath.

Slide the loaf onto a wire rack to cool, then serve with cream cheese and one of Fortnum's finest chutneys.

Herb Scones

These are best eaten freshly made and still warm from the oven. Try them with a slick of butter, some soft goats' cheese or a ribbon of smoked salmon. Use dried rather than fresh herbs in this recipe, as they distribute more evenly through the flour and butter mixture and add a mellow flavour.

Makes 12

260g plain flour, sifted, plus extra, to dust

2 level tsp baking powder

1 tsp salt

65g chilled butter, cubed

2 tsp dried herbs, such as parsley and chives

1 medium egg, beaten

115ml semi-skimmed milk

Preheat the oven to 220°C/425°F/gas mark 7. Line a large baking sheet with baking parchment.

Put the sifted flour into a large bowl and stir in the baking powder and salt. Add the butter and rub in, using your fingers until the mixture resembles breadcrumbs. You can do this in a food processor with a blade, too.

Stir in the herbs evenly. Make a well in the middle of the mixture and pour in the egg. Add the milk and use a knife to quickly mix all the ingredients together. When you've got a rough dough, tip it out onto a floured board and roughly knead – two or three strokes will be enough to bring the mixture together. Shape into a round and pat down two or three times to make a thickness of around 2.5cm.

Flour a 5cm cutter, then cut out rounds of dough and place them on the parchment. (You'll need to reshape the dough twice to make the 12 scones and the last scone you make will be from the smallest piece of dough. This one you can just shape with your hands.)

Bake for 12–15 minutes until just golden, then put on a wire rack to cool.

Fruit Cakes and Tea Breads

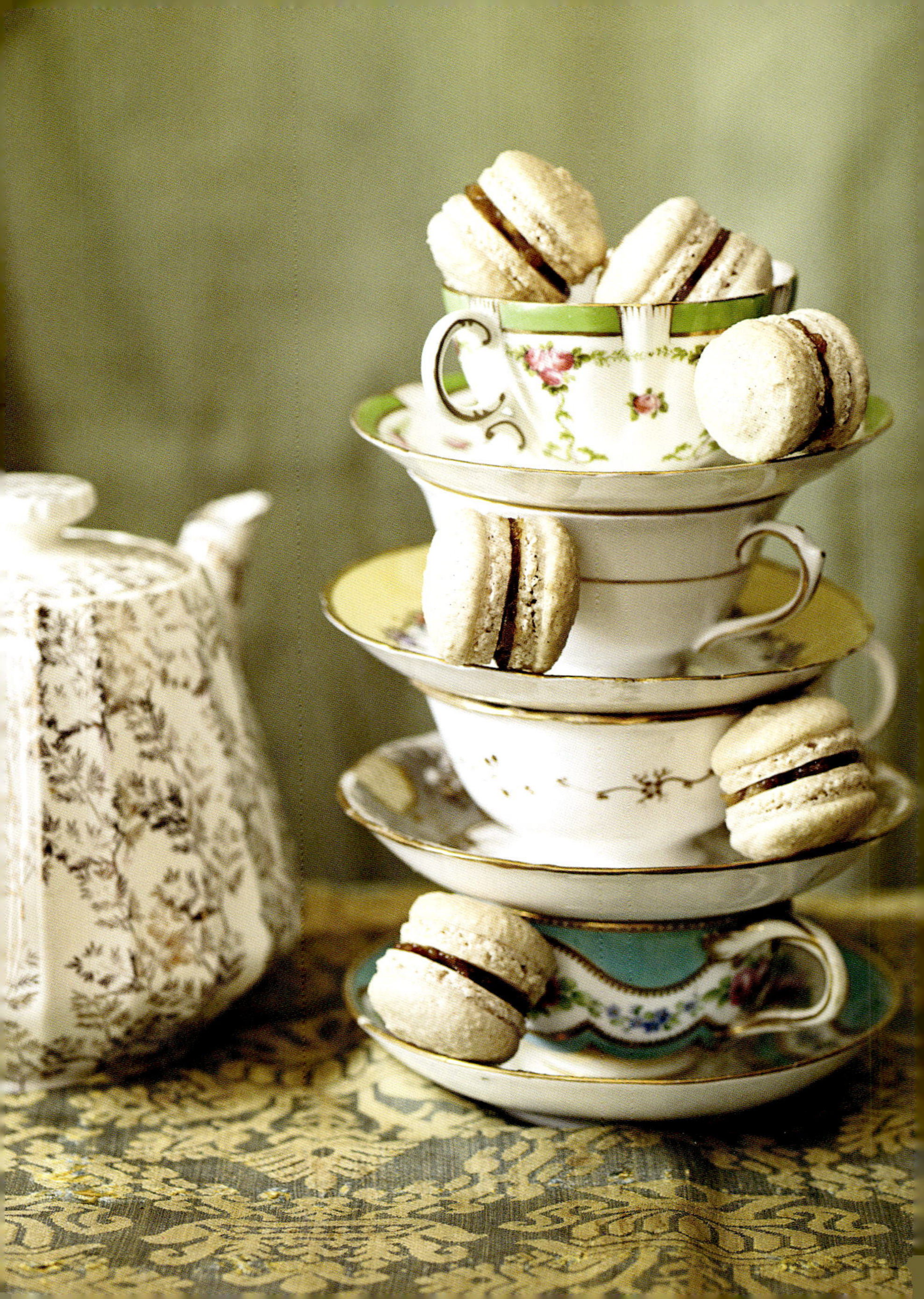

Honey and Date
MACARONS

Makes around 22

For the shells

185g icing sugar

120g ground almonds

100g egg whites (you'll need around 3 medium egg whites)

65g granulated sugar

1 tsp ground cinnamon

For the filling

50g pitted dried dates, soaked overnight in boiling water

1½ tbsp Fortnum & Mason Scottish Heather Honey

½ tbsp rosewater

Line two heavy-based baking sheets with baking parchment. Fit a piping bag with a 2cm round nozzle. Whiz the icing sugar and almonds in a food processor to grind the nuts to a fine powder.

Whisk the egg whites in a spotlessly clean grease-free bowl until stiff peaks form, taking care not to let the mixture become dry. Whisk in the sugar until the mixture is smooth and glossy.

Sift the icing sugar and almond mixture and the cinnamon into a bowl, discarding any bits of almond leftover. Add the meringue mix and fold everything together to get a smooth batter.

Spoon into the piping bag then twist to secure the end. Pipe blobs, about 3-4cm in width onto the parchment-lined trays. Set aside to rest for about 1 hour until the mixture feels dry when you touch it. Preheat the oven to 180°C/350°F/gas mark 4.

Bake the macarons, one sheet at a time, for 10-15 minutes until they barely give when touched.

Slide the parchment onto a wire rack and leave the macarons to cool. Bake the rest and cool as before.

Make the filling. Drain the dates, then chop and put in a small pan with the honey and rosewater. Simmer for around 5 minutes, stirring and beating well to break everything down and make a thickish sauce. Spoon into a bowl and cool.

Take one macaron and spread a little mixture over the base. Top with another macaron about the same size. Continue until all are filled.

STEM GINGER SHORTBREAD *Biscuits*

These crisp biscuits have all the flavour of buttery shortbread but with an extra spicy ginger kick. It is the rice flour that gives them their characteristic crunchy texture.

Makes 20–22 biscuits

100g butter, at room temperature

50g icing sugar

2 tsp Fortnum & Mason Ginger Preserve, No.73

½ tsp ground ginger

110g plain flour, sifted, plus extra to dust

15g rice flour

A little caster sugar, for sprinkling

Preheat the oven to 170°C/325°F/gas mark 3. Line a baking sheet with baking parchment.

Beat the butter in a bowl to soften, then stir in the icing sugar to incorporate it. Stir in the ginger preserve and ground ginger, then gradually work in the flour and rice flour. Knead gently to make a dough.

Lightly flour a board and roll out the dough to about 0.5cm thickness. Use a 5cm cutter to stamp out rounds, re-rolling where necessary, and place them on the prepared baking sheet.

Bake in the oven for 12–15 minutes until pale golden. Prick the tops with a fork to make a pattern, then leave on the baking sheet for a minute or two. Use a palette knife to slide the biscuits onto a wire rack and leave to cool completely. They will firm up as they cool. Sprinkle with a little caster sugar and store in an airtight container for up to three days.

Fortnum's Famous Flavours

Characterised by name and by nature, the theatrical impresario Sir Nigel Playfair became a regular fixture at Fortnum's during the 1920s. He established such close ties with the company that the in-house chefs created a unique marmalade especially for him. The regular preserve on offer didn't quite cut the mustard – it wasn't bitter enough for his taste. So a new recipe was cooked up, consisting of thick-cut peel with a dark bitter flavour. Labeled Sir Nigel's Vintage Marmalade, it continues to be very popular today.

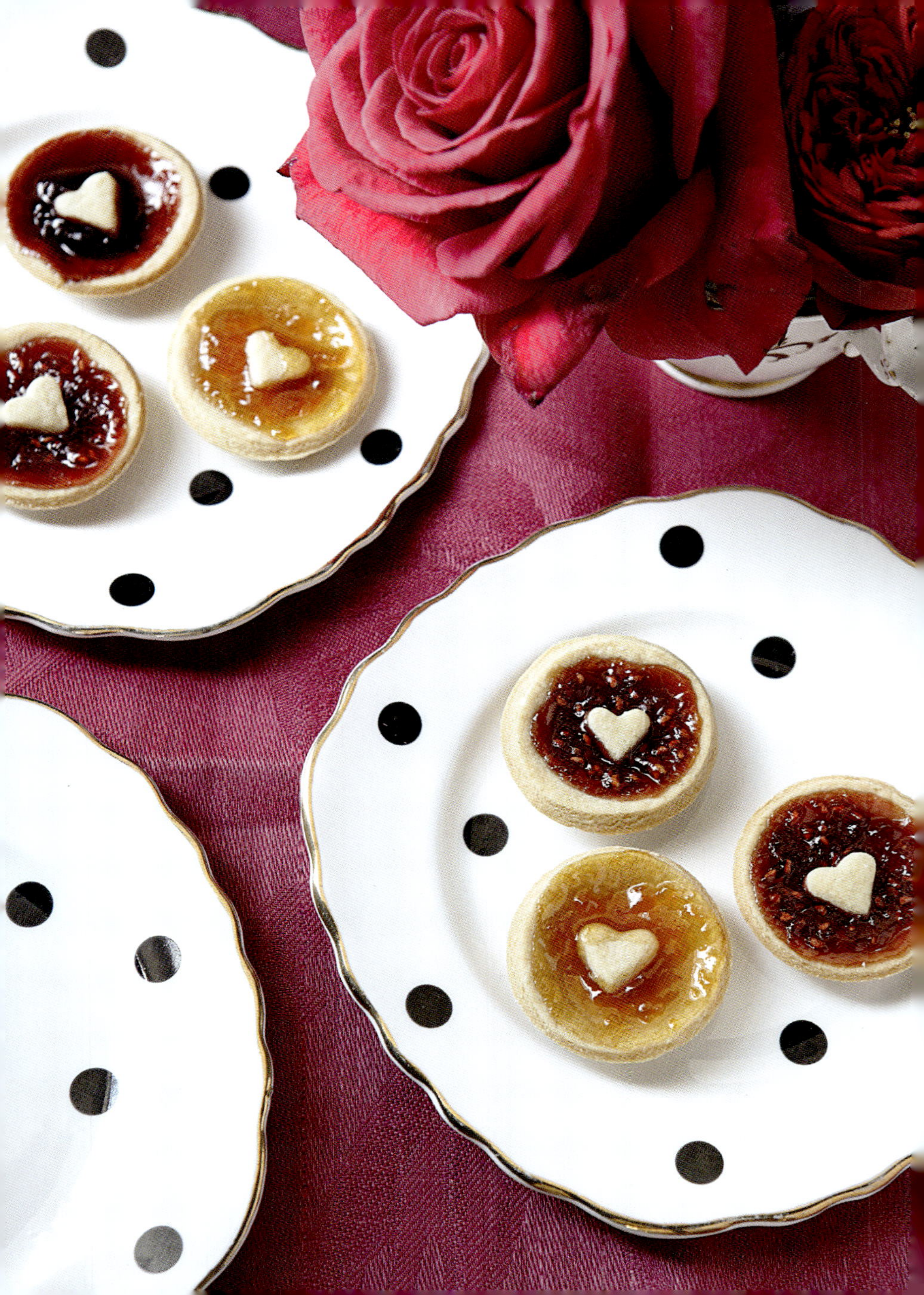

Jam Tarts

These little bite-size treats, made with a sweetened crust, are quick to make and look pretty decorated with a pastry heart.

Makes 24

175g plain flour, sifted

75g butter, cubed and chilled

1 egg yolk

25g icing sugar

A selection of jams, such as Fortnum & Mason Strawberry Preserve, No. 91, Apricot Preserve, No. 98, and Damson Preserve, No. 97

You will need 2 x 12-hole mini-tart tins

Put the flour into a food processor and add the butter. Whiz until the mixture resembles breadcrumbs.

Add the egg yolk, icing sugar and 1 tablespoon cold water then whiz again until the mixture just comes together. Tip out onto a board and quickly knead together to make a dough. Shape into a disc, wrap in clingfilm and chill for at least 30 minutes.

Preheat the oven to 190°C/375°F/gas mark 5. Roll out half the dough on a lightly floured board and cut out 12 rounds, using a 6cm cutter, re-rolling where necessary. Carefully line each hole of the mini-tart tin with a pastry round. With any remaining pastry, stamp out pastry shapes using a cutter.

Spoon the jam into the tarts, top with the pastry hearts, then bake in the oven for about 15 minutes.

Remove the tray from the oven, cool a little, then use a palette knife to carefully remove each tart and place on a wire rack to cool completely.

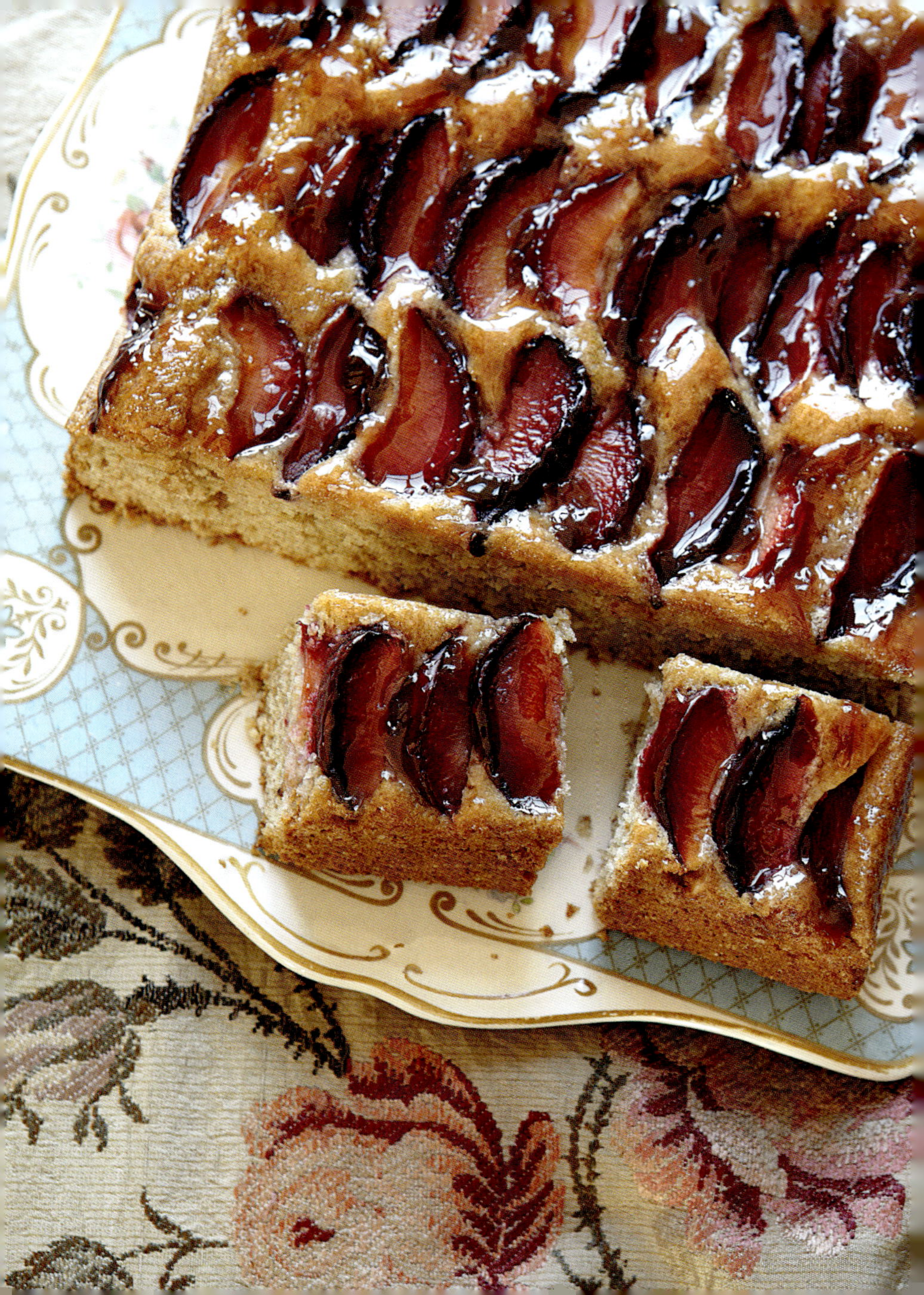

Plum and Hazelnut CAKE

The combination of juicy plums on top of this cake and crunchy hazelnuts within creates a delicious texture and flavour in this tea-time treat. It's glazed in one of Fortnum's finest sweet jelly preserves, which gives it a gorgeous rose-coloured hue.

Serves 8–10

130g butter, plus extra to grease

30g blanched hazelnuts

100g wholemeal flour, sifted

100g golden caster sugar

50g light muscovado sugar

3 medium eggs, beaten

125g self-raising flour, sifted

1 tsp baking powder

Zest and juice of ½ orange

6-8 plums, halved and stoned

2 tbsp Fortnum & Mason Rose Petal Jelly

Preheat the oven to 190°C/375°F/gas mark 5. Grease and line a 20cm loose-bottomed square cake tin with baking parchment.

Put the hazelnuts in a food processor and whiz to chop roughly. Add the wholemeal flour and continue to whiz until the nuts are finely chopped.

Beat the butter, caster sugar and light muscovado sugar in a large bowl until the mixture looks pale creamy. Whisk in the eggs, little by little, until combined.

Fold in the wholemeal flour mixture, the self-raising flour, baking powder, orange zest and juice. Spoon into the tin, spreading the top evenly with a palette knife.

Cut each plum half into five wedges, then arrange them over the top of the cake in rows. Bake in the oven for around 50 minutes until a skewer inserted into the centre comes out clean. Cool in the tin for 5 minutes, then lift out and put on a wire rack to cool completely.

Heat the jelly very gently in a small pan to soften. Remove the paper from the cake and put on a serving plate. Brush the melted jelly over the cake and set aside to cool completely.

Cox's Apple Cream Tea Cake

Cox's apples have a pleasing tart taste and are perfect for this special cake to balance the sweetness. This recipe uses double cream in the batter to give it a wonderful richness.

Serves 10

- 150g softened butter, plus extra for greasing
- 75g golden caster sugar
- 75g Fortnum & Mason cloudy honey
- 3 medium eggs
- 250g self-raising flour, sifted
- 1 tsp baking powder
- 3 small Cox's apples, unpeeled, core removed
- 100ml double cream
- 4 tbsp Fortnum & Mason Apricot Preserve, No. 98
- 1 lemon

Preheat the oven to 190°C/375°F/gas mark 5. Grease and line a 20cm springform cake tin.

Put the butter in a large bowl and add the sugar and honey. Whisk together until the mixture looks pale and creamy.

Continue to beat the mixture, adding one egg at a time, until combined. Fold in the flour and baking powder. Chop two of the apples into small chunks and fold into the mixture with the cream.

Spoon into the prepared tin and level the surface. Finely slice the remaining apple and arrange the slices around the outside, slightly overlapping each other. Bake in the oven for around 1 hour or until a skewer inserted into the centre comes out clean.

Gently warm the preserve in a small pan, then brush it all over the cake. Cool in the tin, then remove and slide onto a plate, removing the greaseproof paper as you do so.

Ginger Parkin

Rolled oats and pinhead oatmeal make this moist tea-time treat delicious and wholesome while Fortnum's Ginger Preserve helps to produce a sticky texture. It's perfect eaten the day it's made but if you keep it for a couple of days it will firm up a bit. Store in an airtight container, wrapped well, and enjoy within five days.

Makes 20 squares

150g softened butter, plus extra for greasing

150g dark muscovado sugar

1 tbsp treacle

2 tbsp whisky

1 tbsp Fortnum & Mason Ginger Preserve, No. 73

3 medium eggs

30g rolled oats

20g pinhead oatmeal

150g self-raising flour, sifted

1 tsp baking powder

2 tsp ground ginger

Preheat the oven to 190°C/375°F/gas mark 5. Grease a 20cm square cake tin and line with greaseproof paper.

Beat the butter, sugar, treacle, whisky and ginger preserve together in a bowl until soft and creamy. Add the eggs, one at a time, and continue to whisk in until combined.

Add the oats, oatmeal, flour, baking powder and ginger and fold everything together lightly. Spoon into the tin and bake for 30 minutes or until a skewer inserted into the centre comes out clean.

Cool in the tin for 5–10 minutes, then remove from the tin and continue to cool on a wire rack.

Madeleines

These moist, light, sponge cakes are made with lemon, honey and the Moroccan spice cardamom, which gives them an exotic, delicate flavour. Madeleines, immortalised in Proust's work *Remembrance of Things Past*, are a favourite of the French, who like to dip them in Fortnum's Tea!

Makes 12

80g unsalted butter, melted and cooled, plus extra to grease

80g self-raising flour, plus extra to dust

50g golden caster sugar

2 medium eggs

30g Fortnum & Mason set honey

½ tsp baking powder

Zest of ½ lemon

Seeds from 2 cardamom pods, ground

Icing sugar, to dust

Preheat the oven to 190°C/375°F/gas mark 5. Generously grease a 12-mould madeleine tin and dust generously with flour.

Whisk together the sugar, eggs and honey in a bowl until moussey and a ribbon-like trail is left when you lift the whisks. In a separate bowl, mix together the flour with the baking powder. Add half each of the butter and the flour mixture to the eggs and sugar and fold in. Add the remaining butter and flour mixture with the lemon zest and ground cardamom and fold everything together carefully.

Divide the mixture among the moulds and bake for about 10 minutes until cooked. Cool for a few minutes in the tin, then use a palette knife to lift the madeleines out carefully and place them on a wire rack to cool. Dust with icing sugar, to serve.

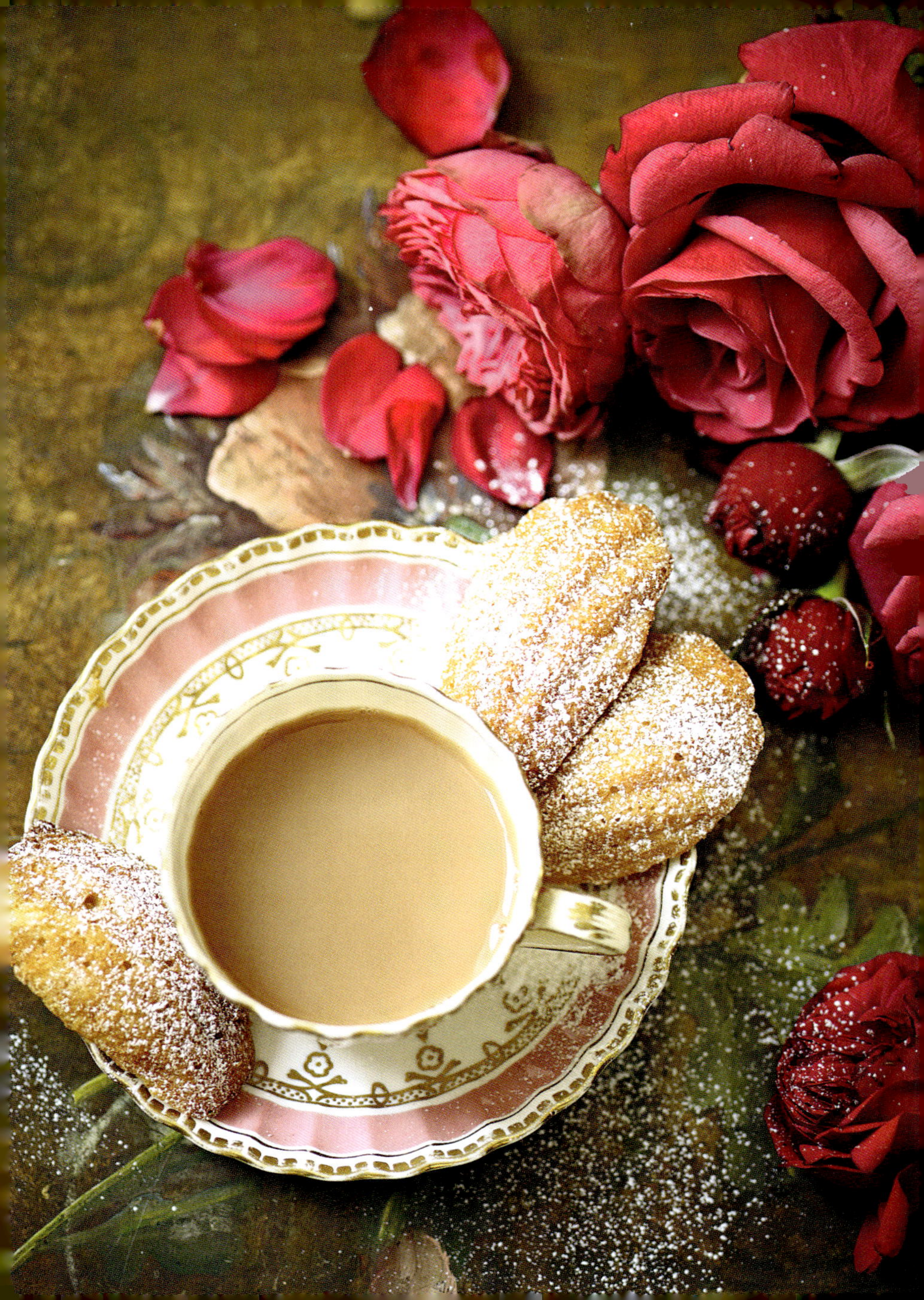

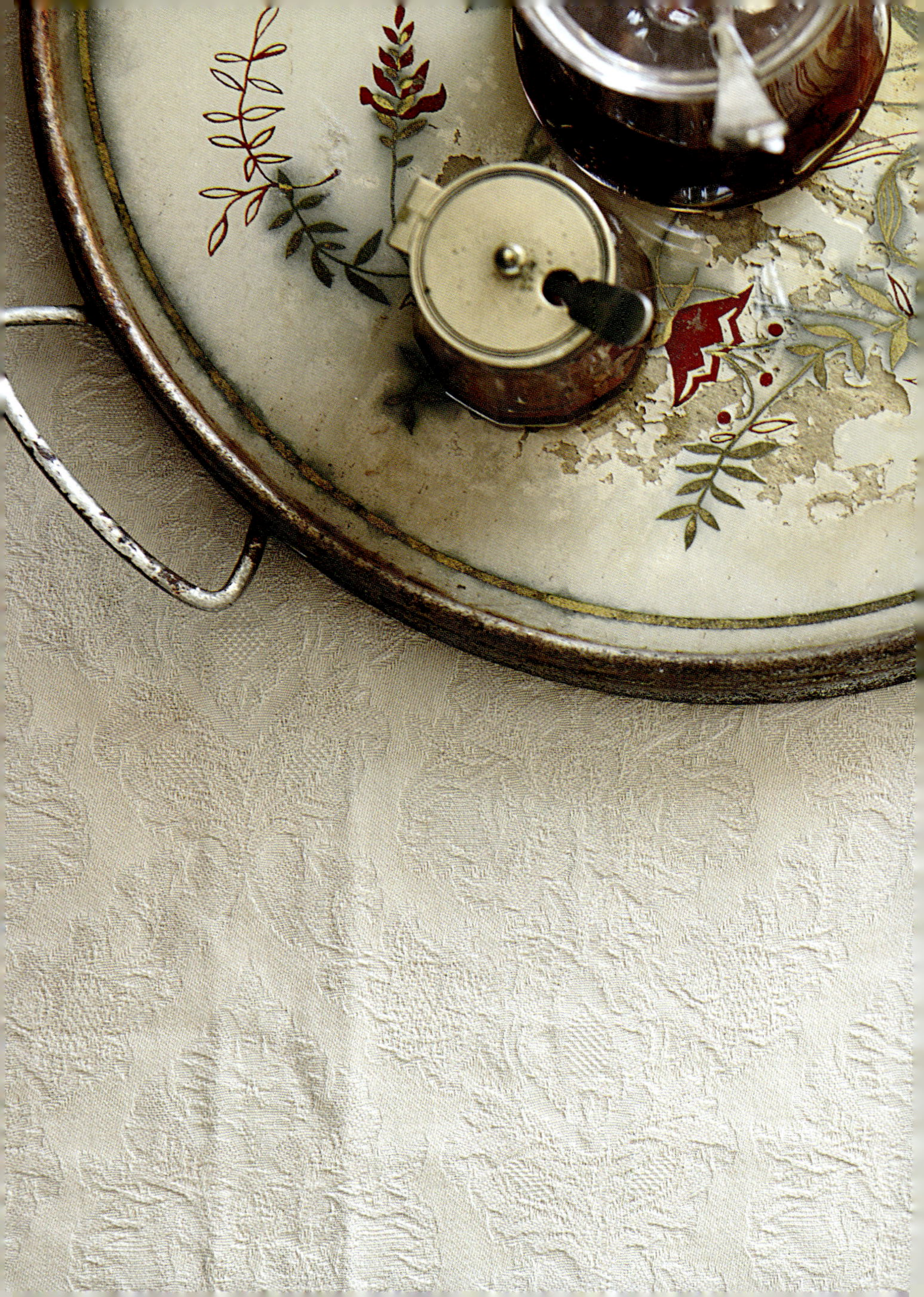

Preserves

THE RULES OF PRESERVING

Preserving fruit and vegetables is the great way to make them last all-year round if you have a homegrown glut or when they're at their seasonal prime. To get the best results you need a few essential pieces of equipment.

KEY EQUIPMENT

Use large stainless steel or lined copper or aluminium preserving pans. They're large enough to allow jams, jellies and marmalades to cook without boiling over and ensure that the liquid in chutneys evaporates evenly. For smaller quantities, stainless steel saucepans or lined aluminium pans can be used. You need a jelly bag and stand if you are making jellies.

You also need a selection of jam jars with lids. Jars must always be sterilised before filling with preserves; to do this, wash them first in soapy water then rinse well. Place them upturned on a baking sheet and dry out in an oven preheated to 130°C/275°F/gas mark 1 for 10–15 minutes. Both the jars and the preserves should be hot while potting.

JAMS, JELLIES AND MARMALADES

For jams, jellies or marmalades, fruit should be just ripe, otherwise their setting quality may be impaired. Any bruised parts should be removed, except in the case of chutney when bruised fruit, such as windfalls, can still be used in the recipe, as it will cook down to have the same appearance as the other fruit.

When making jams and jellies, test for a set. To do this, place two or three saucers in the freezer to chill quickly. Take the pan off the heat, otherwise the jam may become overboiled, and spoon a little of the mixture onto a saucer. Return the saucer to the freezer for one minute to cool quickly. Take out of the freezer and run your finger through the middle. If it wrinkles, it's ready to pot.

CURDS

A curd is not a traditional preserve in the true sense, as it is made from fresh butter and eggs. It should be made in small quantities and refrigerated at once then eaten quickly.

CHUTNEYS AND PICKLES

Chutneys need to be simmered slowly, in wide, open pans over a low heat to allow even evaporation. They are ready when the mixture is thick and sauce-like and no excess liquid remains. The length of time it takes to cook the chutney will depend on the initial quantity of ingredients used and the depth of the pan, but it can be between 1 and 4 hours.

To pot chutneys and pickles, spoon the hot mixture into sterilised jars and cover immediately with vinegar-proof tops, such as lids with a plastic lining. Jams, jellies, chutneys and pickles can all be kept for up to a year if potted and stored in a cool dark place.

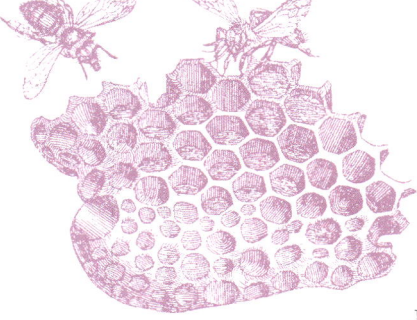

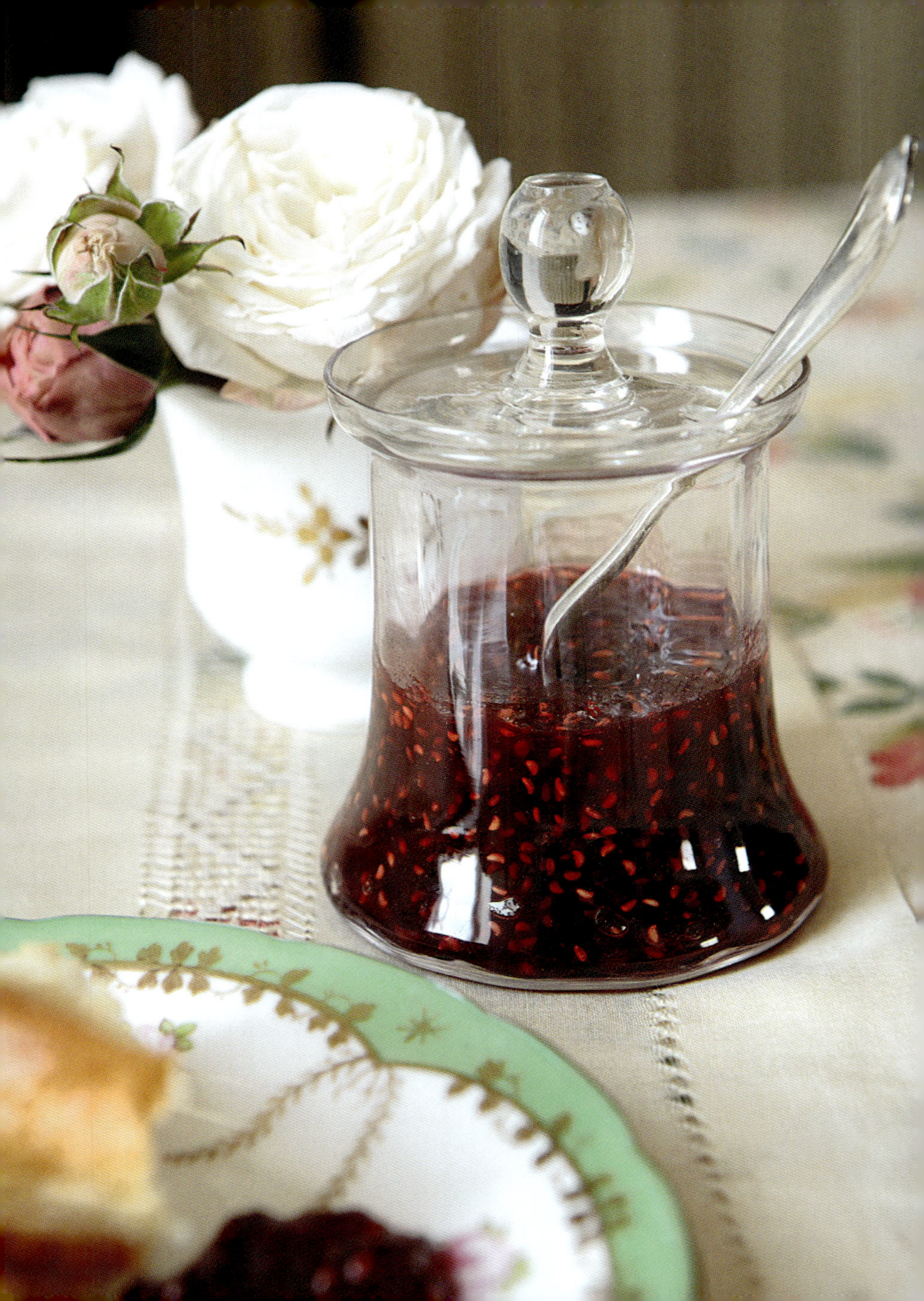

Raspberry Jam

Prolong the taste of summer in this rich conserve made with seasonal berries. Spoon it onto freshly buttered teacakes in an indulgent afternoon tea in the sun, or enjoy it for breakfast on granary toast. It is also excellent in our recipe for Scottish Raspberry Trifle (page 85).

Makes around 1.4kg

1kg raspberries, washed

50ml cold water

1kg unrefined granulated sugar

1 tbsp Chambord raspberry liqueur (optional)

A knob of butter

Place the raspberries in a preserving pan with the cold water. Bring to the boil and simmer for around 20 minutes until the fruit has softened into a pool of mashed-up berries.

Add the sugar and heat gently, stirring all the time, to dissolve the sugar. Bring to a rolling boil and cook for about 15–20 minutes or until setting point is reached. Stir in the butter, which will help to disperse any froth on the top, and the raspberry liqueur, if using.

Pot into sterilised jars, seal and label. The jam is ready to enjoy straight away. Once opened, store in the fridge.

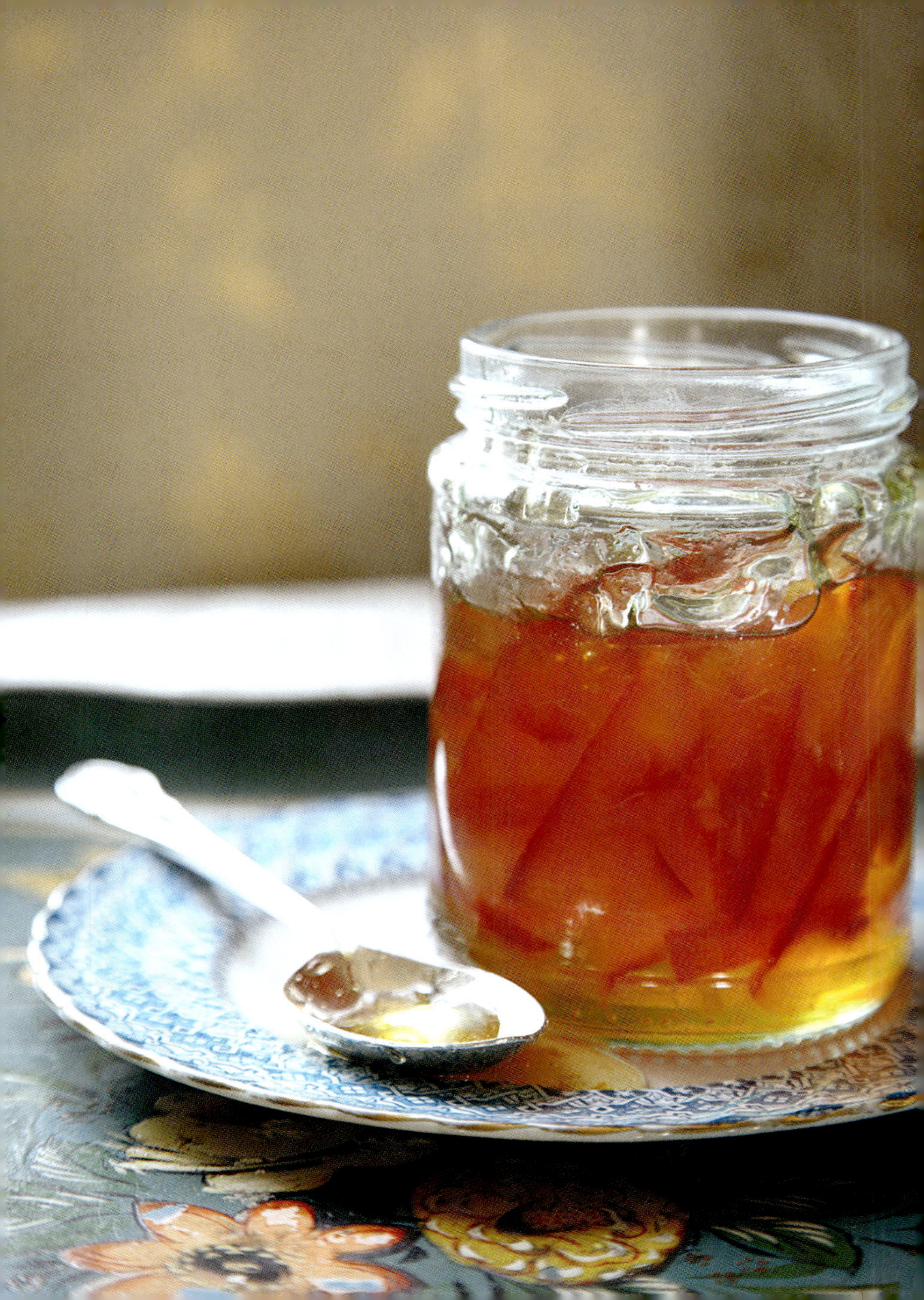

Seville Orange Marmalade

The bitter quality of Spanish Seville oranges is the best choice for making this classic preserve but they are in season for just a short time at the beginning of every year. You can freeze the fruit for up to a year, however this reduces setting quality so use only two-thirds of the usual sugar requirement. Spicy stem ginger has been added here, which adds a gentle warmth.

Makes around 2kg

750g Seville oranges, washed

1kg golden granulated sugar

500g demerara sugar

3 balls stem ginger in syrup, drained and finely chopped

Halve the oranges and squeeze out the juice. If you use an electric juicer, it halves the time and removes all the pith and pips, too. If you are squeezing by hand, after extracting the juice, use a spoon to scoop out all of the pith and pips. Place them in a square of muslin and secure with string.

Finely slice the rind and place it in a preserving pan with the juice. Tie the muslin bag to the handle and let it sit on the bottom of the pan. Add 2.3 litres cold water. Bring to the boil then simmer gently for 1–2 hours until the rind is soft and liquid has reduced by about half.

Stir in the sugars and ginger and heat gently to dissolve. Put a saucer in the freezer to chill quickly.

Increase the heat and boil gently for 15 minutes until setting point is reached. To test for a set, take the pan off the heat and put a spoonful of the marmalade on the chilled saucer. Draw your finger across the marmalade. If it wrinkles, it is set. If not, continue to boil for 5 minutes until the setting point is reached.

Spoon into hot sterilised jars, top with a waxed disc, then seal with a lid. The marmalade will keep, sealed, for up to a year in a cool place.

Lemon AND LIME CURD

This exotic-flavoured curd is perfect spread between the layers of a Victoria sponge as an alternative to jam, or folded into whipped double cream to marry together two meringue halves. There is a perfect balance between the passion fruit and lime in this, so it is sweet and tart in equal proportions.

Makes one 575g jar

Zest and juice of 2 limes

Zest and juice of 1 lemon

3 medium eggs

175g golden caster sugar

100g butter, cubed and chilled

Place the lime zest and juice in a large heatproof bowl. Add the lemon zest and juice, eggs, sugar and butter. Use a wooden spoon to stir the mixture to break up the eggs.

Place the bowl over a pan of simmering water, making sure the base doesn't touch the water. Cook over a medium heat, stirring all the time, until the mixture thickens.

Strain into a clean bowl to remove any cooked white from the egg. Pot, while still hot, into a clean sterilised jar. Allow to cool, then refrigerate and enjoy within two weeks.

Preserving Blooms

Fortnum & Mason preserves are a treasure chest of delights, but the jewels in the crown have to be the dark-pink-hued Rose Petal Jelly and Strawberry & Rose Preserve. The main ingredient, a delightful damask rose, is grown in a single garden in Oxfordshire – the exact location of which remains a closely-guarded secret. These exclusive flowers are freshly picked by hand to protect the delicate petals, and only in the late afternoon when their fragrance is at its best. After being 'riddled' to remove the bugs, whole petals are used to make the unique preserves.

There's no waste either, as even broken petals have value, and are used to create the aromatic Rose Petal Vinegar. This vinegar is delicious in salad dressings and over carpaccio of scallops, where the tartness of the vinegar and perfumed aroma of the petals sing, or drop a splash or two into cake batter to transform a Victoria sponge. Fortnum's is keen to support this small artisan producer, and others like it, to help sustain cottage industries in the same way it has always done since the store opened its doors in 1707.

Apricot Jam

Preserve the best of the summer's stone fruit in this fragrant and fruity jam. It is perfect with scones and clotted cream, or use in place of traditional strawberry to fill a Victoria sponge cake.

Makes around 1.7kg

1kg fresh apricots

1 vanilla pod

1kg unrefined granulated sugar

Juice of ½ lemon

1 tbsp kirsch

Halve the apricots and discard the stones, then cut in half again. Place the apricot quarters into a preserving pan with 300ml cold water. Bring to the boil, then simmer gently until the fruit is soft and pulpy.

Place the vanilla pod on a board and use a knife to cut along its length. Run a table knife along the pod to extract the seeds, then add the seeds to the preserving pan. Add the sugar and lemon juice and heat gently to dissolve the sugar.

Bring to the boil and cook for 10–15 minutes or until setting point is reached. Pot into sterilised jars, seal and label. The jam is ready to eat straight away. Once opened, store in the fridge and enjoy within one month.

GRAPE AND *Apple Jelly*

This jewel-like claret-coloured jelly is made by cooking the fruit with red wine vinegar, which gives it an acidic edge to any resulting sweetness. Serve with goats' cheese and nutty granary rolls, white meats or stir into a meat gravy to provide a balance of flavour.

Makes around 1.4kg

1kg whole cooking apples, such as Bramley

1kg red grapes

600ml red wine vinegar

Granulated sugar

Chop the apples, leaving the core intact, and place them in a preserving pan. Add the grapes and 600ml cold water. Bring to the boil and simmer for about 30 minutes until the apples have softened and the fruit has cooked down to a pulp.

Add the vinegar, bring to the boil again, and simmer for 5 minutes. Spoon into a jelly bag, set over a bowl and allow the liquid to strain into it for at least 8 hours.

Measure and note the quantity of the liquid and pour it into a preserving pan. Add 450g granulated sugar for each 600ml liquid. Bring to the boil and cook for at least 10 minutes or until setting point is reached.

Pot into sterilised jars, seal and label. The jelly is ready to eat straight away or can be stored in a cool dark place for up to six months. Once opened, store in the fridge and enjoy within one month.

Spiced Apple and Tomato Chutney

This chutney is the perfect way to preserve a glut of tomatoes at the end of summer and an early harvest of cooking apples. The tart acidity of the apples combines well with the sweet tomatoes but its special spicy flavour comes from the chilli, cumin seeds and black pepper.

Makes around 1.7kg

1kg cooking apples (such as Bramley), peeled, chopped and cored

2 medium onions, peeled and chopped

1kg tomatoes, quartered and core removed

2 fresh red chillies, finely chopped

1 tsp cumin seeds

1 litre white wine vinegar

375g demerara sugar

1 tsp each salt and coarsely ground black pepper

Place all the ingredients in a preserving pan and bring gently to the boil. Reduce the heat to its lowest setting and simmer gently for around 2 hours, stirring every now and then to stop the mixture sticking to the bottom of the pan. The chutney is ready when it is thick, saucy and no excess liquid remains.

Pot into sterilised jars, seal and label. Allow to mature for at least one month. The chutney can be stored in a cool, dark place for up to a year. Once opened, store in the fridge and enjoy within one month.

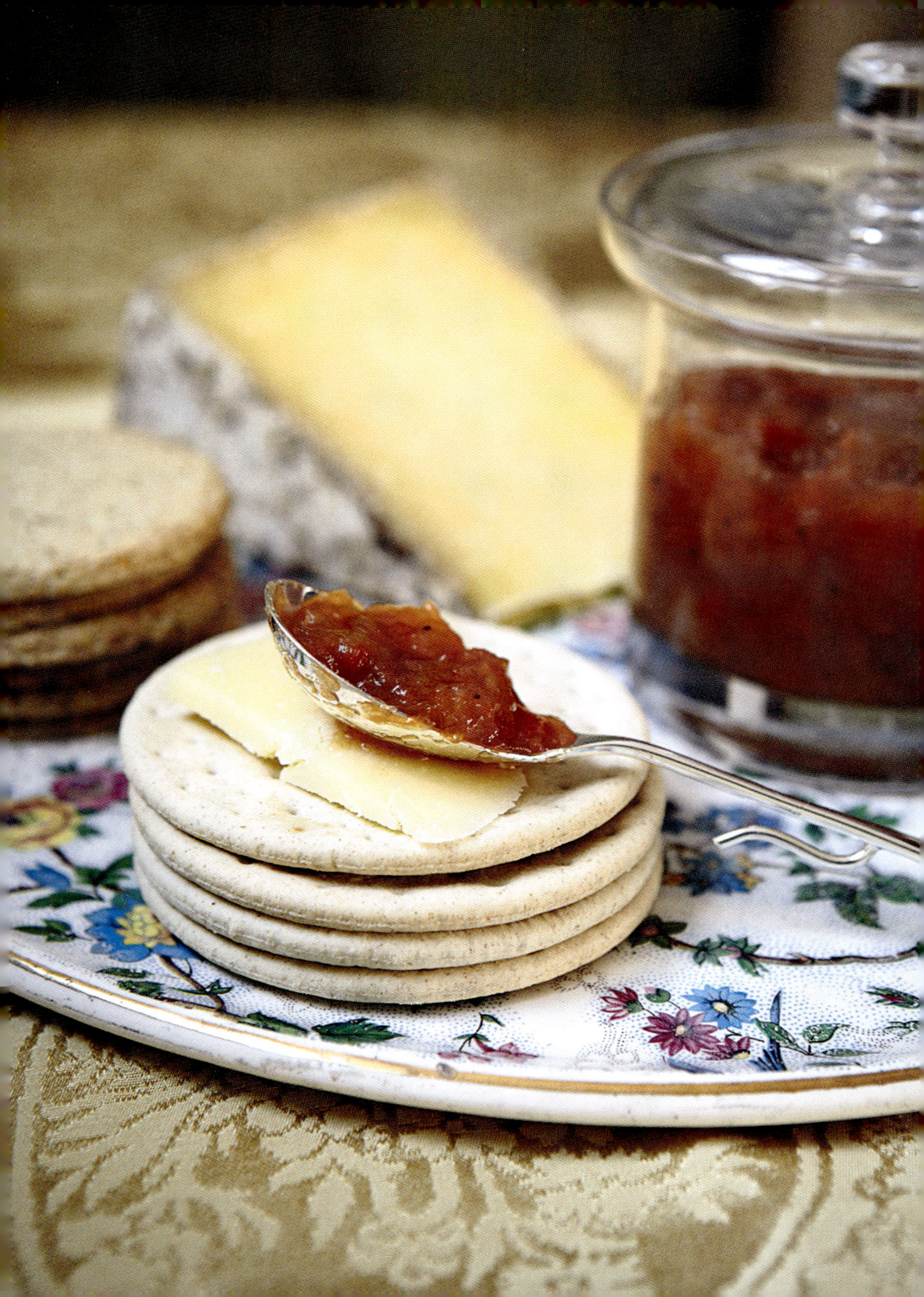

Hot Mango Chutney

Sweet, soft mangoes are cooked down with myriad aromatic spices to create this fiery condiment. Serve with lamb, chicken or vegetable curry.

Makes around 1.4kg

- 20 cardamom pods
- 2 tsp chilli flakes
- 1 tsp turmeric
- 1 tbsp cayenne pepper
- 2 tsp cumin seeds
- 3 fresh red chillies, halved and seeded and finely chopped
- 2kg mangoes, peeled, stoned and finely diced
- 600ml cider vinegar
- Juice of 2 limes
- 1 large onion, finely chopped
- 500g light muscovado sugar
- 2 tsp salt

Split the cardamom pods and put the seeds in a coffee mill. Add the chilli flakes, turmeric, cayenne pepper and cumin seeds and whiz to grind to a powder.

Put the spice mixture, chillies, diced mango, vinegar, lime juice and onion into a preserving pan. Bring to the boil, then simmer for 15 minutes until the mango has softened.

Add the sugar and salt and stir in. Bring to the boil, then turn down the heat to its lowest setting and simmer for 45 minutes until the mixture is thick and saucy. It is important to stir it from time to time, particularly towards the end of cooking, to stop it from sticking to the bottom of the pan.

Pot into sterilised jars, seal and label. Allow to mature for at least one month in a cool, dark place. Once opened, store in the fridge and eat within one month.

Fortnum's
FLORENTINE CHUTNEY

Based on one of Fortnum's best-selling preserves this mildly spiced condiment is rich with dried fruit and is best served with cold cuts of meat or a chunk of good Cheddar cheese.

Makes around 2kg

500g dried apricots, finely chopped

275g sultanas

150g dried dates, chopped

1.65 litres water

600ml white wine vinegar

125g demerara sugar

50g flaked almonds

50g crystallised ginger, chopped

½ tbsp Dijon mustard

1 tsp cayenne pepper

1 tsp salt

Put all the ingredients in a non-metallic container and set aside to soak for at least 8 hours.

Tip the soaked mixture into a preserving pan and place over a medium heat. Bring gently to the boil, then turn down the heat and simmer for around 1 hour and 40 minutes until the fruit has softened and the chutney has cooked down. The mixture will look thick and saucy.

Pot into sterilised jars, seal and label. Allow to mature for at least one month in a cool, dark place. Once opened, store in the fridge and eat within one month.

Piccalilli

Tender chunks of cauliflower, pepper and onion are pickled in a mustard and spice sauce in this classic British pickle. The tart, acidic taste makes this a traditional accompaniment to baked ham or meat terrines, to cut through the rich flavours.

Makes around 1.1kg

- 1 small cauliflower
- 1 each red and green pepper
- 1 onion
- 140g salt
- 600ml distilled malt vinegar
- 5 gherkins, finely chopped
- 1 tbsp capers
- 75g unrefined granulated sugar
- 1 tsp English mustard powder
- ½ tsp ground ginger
- A pinch of ground cloves
- 20g plain flour
- 2 tsp turmeric

Prepare the vegetables. Remove the leaves from the cauliflower (the small inner leaves can be steamed for an accompaniment to another meal) and break into small florets.

Halve and seed each pepper and finely chop. Peel and finely chop the onion. Layer the vegetables in a sealable container, sprinkling each layer with the salt. Add 1.4 litres water, cover with the lid and leave overnight.

Drain the vegetables and rinse well.

Pour 450ml vinegar into a large pan. Add the rinsed vegetables, the gherkins and capers and bring gently to the boil. Simmer for 10–12 minutes until the vegetables are just tender.

Pour the remaining vinegar into a bowl. Add the sugar, mustard powder, ground ginger and cloves, plain flour and turmeric. Use a wooden spoon to blend all the ingredients together.

Pour into the pan, bring to the boil and continue to cook for 2–3 minutes until the sauce has thickened.

Spoon into sterilised jars, seal and label. Allow to mature for at least one month in a cool, dark place. Once opened, store in the fridge and enjoy within one month.

Index

apple
    Cox's, cream tea cake 106
    and grape jelly 121
    and tomato spiced chutney 122–3
    and walnut strudel tart 82
apricot
    glaze 80–1
    jam 120

bacon, game and pistachio terrine 44–5
beef and stout puff pastry pie 56–7
berries, with Prosecco jelly 90–1
bread
    granary and rye rolls 94–5
    seeded soda 94
brioche, toasted, garlic mushrooms on 50
bruschetta, pear and Stilton 40–1

cakes
    chocolate and prune 79
    Cox's apple cream tea 106
    ginger Parkin 107
    Madeleines 116–17
    plum and hazelnut 104–5
carrots, with honey, orange and sesame 69
cheese
    fruit 17, 23
    Montgomery's Cheddar and onion tart 72
    twice-baked Lancashire soufflé 73
    see also pecorino; Stilton
cheesecake, lemon and lime 86–7
cherry, morello, and port sauce 63
chicken, honey roast, and shallots 64–5
chicory salad 40–1
chocolate and prune cake 79
chutney 13, 22, 113
    apple and tomato spiced 122–3
    Fortnum's Florentine 125
    hot mango 124
    mango 51, 124
contemporary tastes 22–3
courgette, pine nut, rocket & pecorino salad 39
crab, spicy salad 47
crème caramel, honey 83
cucumber sauce, warm 66–7
curds 12, 113
    lemon 20–1

lemon and lime 118
custard, whisky 76–7

date and honey macarons 98–9
duck breasts & port & morello cherry sauce 63

Elsenham 16
equipment 112

fig, honey and spiced roast lamb 58–9
French beans & mustard & hazelnut dressing 70–1
fruit cheeses 17, 23

game and pistachio terrine 44–5
garlic mushrooms on toasted brioche 50
ginger
    Parkin 107
    stem, shortbread biscuits 100
glaze, apricot 80–1
grape and apple jelly 121
gravadlax, homemade 42–3

ham
    marmalade-glazed 60–1
    Parma, and pork tenderloin 62
hazelnut
    and mustard dressing 70–1
    and plum cake 104–5
history of preserving 10–16
honey 17, 25–35
    crème caramel 83
    and date macarons 98–9
    figs, and spiced roast lamb 58–9
    orange and sesame carrots 69
    roast chicken, & caramelised shallots 64–5
honeycomb 28

ice cream, lavender 88

jam 12, 15–16, 20, 113
    apricot 120
    extra 12, 17
    Marrow and Ginger 15–16
    raspberry 114–15
    rose petal 119
    strawberry 17, 20
    tarts 102–3

Jam Temple, The 23
jars 101, 112
jelly 12, 15, 20, 23, 113
    grape and apple 121
    Prosecco, with summer fruits 90–1
    rose petal 119

lamb, spiced roast, figs and honey 58–9
lavender ice cream 88
lemon
    curd 20–1
    and lime cheesecake 86–7
    and lime curd 118

macarons, honey and date 98–9
Madeleines 108–9
mango 14
    chutney 51, 124
    hot chutney 124
Manuka Honey 35
marmalade 12, 17, 19, 78, 113
    -glazed ham 60–1
    puddings, & whisky custard 76–7
    Seville orange 116–17
mushroom(s), garlic, on toasted brioche 50
mustard 13, 17, 21
    and hazelnut dressing 70–1
    pastry bites 52–3

Parkin, ginger 107
Parma ham and pork tenderloin 62
parsnip and thyme soup 38
pastry 80–1
peach, poached 89
pear
    & Stilton bruschetta & chicory salad 40–1
    tart, with apricot glaze 80–1
pecorino, courgette, pine nut & rocket salad 39
pepper relish 46
pheasant, game and pistachio terrine 44–5
piccalilli 14, 22, 126
pickles 13, 22–3, 113
pie, beef and stout puff pastry 56–7
plum and hazelnut cake 104–5
pork
    belly, game and pistachio terrine 44–5
    tenderloin, with Parma ham 62
potato, new, and spinach warm salad 68
preserves 111–26
Prosecco jelly with summer fruits 90–1
prune and chocolate cake 79

rabbit, game and pistachio terrine 44–5
raspberry
    jam 17, 114–15
    Scottish trifle 84–5
relish 13
    pepper 46
rocket, pecorino, courgette & pine nut salad 39
rose preserves 119
rules of preserving 112–13

salad
    chicory 40–1
    pecorino, courgette, pine nut & rocket 39
    spicy crab 47
    warm new potato and spinach 68
salmon
    homemade gravadlax 42–3
    with a warm cucumber sauce 66–7
scallops, pan-fried, honey, soy and chilli 47
scones, herb 97
setting preserves 113
shallot(s), caramelised 64–5
shortbread biscuits, stem ginger 100
soufflé, twice-baked Lancashire cheese 73
soup, parsnip and thyme 38
spinach
    and new potato warm salad 68
    and squash terrine with pepper relish 46
Stilton & pear bruschetta & chicory salad 40–1
strawberry jam 17, 20
strudel tart, apple and walnut 82

tarts
    apple and walnut strudel 82
    jam 110–11
    Montgomery's Cheddar and onion 72
    pear, with apricot glaze 80–1
terrine
    game and pistachio 44–5
    spinach and squash 46
tomato and apple spiced chutney 122–3
trifle, Scottish raspberry 84–5

walnut and apple strudel tart 82
whisky custard 76–7